D0002506

Michael Werner

What Can You Believe if You Don't Believe in God?

Humanist Press

What Can You Believe in if You Don't Believe in God?

Michael Werner

Table of Contents

This book is dedicated to my family who have loved and supported me. It is also dedicated to the countless individuals who have added to our Humanist garden over the centuries. All that I have recounted in this book are the gifts of their efforts to better our world in myriad ways, courageously, wisely, intelligently, compassionately and with great effort.

Preface

"We make our world significant by the courage of our questions and the depth of our answers." – Carl Sagan

This book is for anyone who has ever questioned their belief in God, religion and the supernatural, as well as those who already are nontheists. Doubt is only the first step in the search for a whole story of life. You may wonder, "What can I believe if I don't believe in God?" All the big questions then open up, such as, "What is truth?" "How can nonbelievers be moral?" "How shall I best live?" and "What shall I hope for?"

Philosophical questioning begins a wonderful adventure. At the age of ten or eleven, I started down that path. I was sitting alone in the back of a church, praying to a supposedly caring God to relieve my sufferings, but I received no response. It suddenly occurred to me that I didn't know what I was talking about—and neither did anyone else. I saw fault lines in all my beliefs, from the notion of the Trinity, to the idea of just having ungrounded faith, and, most important, to the problem of evil in the world. I made a vow then to learn the truth about life, no matter what. If that led me to hell, so be it, but I would commit myself to seeking truth no matter where it led me.

Instinctively, I also knew my quest would take years. It indeed did take a long time and with persistent effort. I was not really comfortable with my beliefs until I was almost forty. I credit many of the early Humanist pioneers for their guidance and insights, which opened windows into the depths of what it means to be really human. This has meant everything to me. The "dangerous" adventure I chose in my youth has been an exhilarating and ultimately satisfying ride.

Because many other books do an excellent job of presenting the fallacy of supernatural beliefs and the problems with religion, I will only briefly cover these issues. I hope to provide the next step: some moorings and practical answers. My book is a primer on Humanism, but I will attempt to go into more depth about some of the more fundamental philosophical questions.

I can recommend some other excellent primers. These include the classic *The Philosophy of Humanism* by Corliss Lamont; *Creating Change Through Humanism* by Roy Speckhardt, *Eupraxophy, Living without Religion* by Paul Kurtz; *Humanism* by Stephen Law; *Humanism* by Peter Cave; *Good Without God* by Greg Epstein; and *Reason and Reverence* by William R. Murry.

In many cases I can only provide an alternative viewpoint. Nowhere will any of us find absolute certainty or simple formulas for living. Some answers are evolving, unknown, enigmatic, or ambiguous.

There are many ways to live the good life with or without religion. Sometimes my personal answers to vexing questions will differ from other Humanists' equally personal answers. This is only as it should be since I never will claim to be a final or absolute authority. Still, unlike many within the philosophical community, I will not shirk from standing up for certain beliefs. What you will find here are answers that may help you on your own bold journey.

Some of this undoubtedly will be difficult. I am not one who will offer you simple answers or appeal to the lowest common denominator. I would not offer simple or trite phrases such as "Just be good" or "Just believe in the evidence," even if they are true. That is because the issues of life are complex and require serious consideration if we are not to be superficial and misleading.

I find, as Socrates did, that there are two big questions in life: What is true? And how should we live? Right now you may be scared of falling into some sort of nihilistic relativism. I assure you, however, that most if not all of your questions have satisfying answers. Have courage that the journey is worth it, and that ultimately it can forge a foundation for living that is stronger, truer, and more ennobling than any religion can offer.

1

Why Humanism?

You are reading this book, perhaps, because you have taken a path away from your religious faith or have serious doubts about it. You probably also have a lot of questions and fears. This book is meant to share with you the insights of others about what you might believe and how you might live. You may feel shorn of support and feel a bit like a pariah. On the other hand, you may relish being the outsider and view this transformation as an exciting adventure.

I am amazed at what I hear about what it means to be a nonbeliever. To be an Atheist, Agnostic, Humanist, Freethinker or anything that sows doubts about the existence of God would seem to put us in the category of everything from Satanists, Communists and moral relativists to nasty cynics and hate mongers. We are possibly in league with the devil. Wow. This amount of evil is a hard load to carry.

On the other hand, maybe you never were religious and a belief in God is just not important to you. Nevertheless, you are wondering, "What can I believe in if I don't believe in God?" Another way to pose the question is, "What can I count on, but also what breathes power, meaning, energy, and wholeness into my life?"

Why Humanism? Because we want to devote our lives to profound ideals. We want to answer the fundamental questions of existence. We are looking for passionate life commitments beyond our own needs. We are looking for ideals born of conscious reflection in the glaring light of knowledge. As the progressive educator John Dewey wrote, "We are looking for those ideals and ends so inclusive that they unify the self." We desire a "North Star" to guide us.

According to the Religious Landscape Study completed by the Pew Research Center in 2016, those who call themselves nonreligious are the largest and fastest growing "religious" segment of our society. Around 25 percent of the total population in the United States are religious "nones." That is more than all the Jews, Muslims, Buddhists, Hindus, and Unitarians combined. Our numbers are larger than the Catholics. Among young adults, ages 18-29, 39 percent are religiously unaffiliated. Some of those are "spiritual, but not religious". Atheists altogether account for between 3 and 6 percent of the population. Another 6 percent are agnostic.

Interestingly, polling depends on the questions asked. If you ask, "Do you believe in God?" anywhere from 12 to 18 percent say they don't. It appears that the word "atheist" has a negative connotation that keeps people from expressing their real views on the supernatural. If you feel alone, remember that, on average, of any 100 people on your street, 25 are non-religious. Among young people, that ratio is four of every ten. You are not alone.

We are there next to you at work, in the charities you may belong to, and in your families. We are largely invisible, as we tend not to tout our opinions or evangelize. Many of us are afraid to speak up and some of us couldn't care less. Things are changing, however, and we are learning to share our own world view, believing we have something really great to guide us, to nurture us, to integrate our lives, to bring meaning and purpose. We call this whole naturalistic life stance of beliefs, values and practices Humanism.

Many say that if you don't believe in God then you must not believe in anything. My atheism is more than what I don't believe; I have a whole naturalistic world view called Humanism that illuminates my life. My atheism merely says I don't believe in God, but it says nothing of why I don't believe or how certain that nonbelief is. Most Humanists are pretty certain there is no God because we don't see any credible evidence for God's existence. We believe that even finding a definition can seem nonsensical. Moreover, there is a lot of evidence to the contrary that most of our notions of God are just man-made myths. There are some abstract notions of God we will consider later.

Humanism is an evolving tradition. It reflects what we can best believe and what we can best value. Humanism is a comprehensive world view that speaks to everything we encounter. It is an evolving life stance that says this world is all there is, and is enough. It's enough to gain truth and meaning, tell us about our origins, and fill us with awe and wonder. Humanism shows us what there is in the world, and how to best live our lives.

The *Humanist Manifesto III* summarizes this idea when it says, "Humanism is a progressive life stance that, without supernaturalism, affirms our ability and responsibility to lead meaningful, ethical lives capable of adding to the greater good of humanity." That is as good as any definition I have seen.

Humanists traditionally support open-minded critical thinking about what is believable. We reject dogmatic certainty, as it is a tomb of the mind. We like to keep our minds and hearts open, but at some point the evidence is overwhelming that the best way to live our lives is to see the natural world as all that there is. To believe that is also to believe that there is no evidence for the existence of gods, devils, heaven, hell, ghosts, fairies, unicorns, etc. Jettisoning the supernatural, we can develop a deepened sense of what makes a difference in making the good life.

We have found that science and reason are the best, even if not the only, tools to explain and predict the world. Science and reason stand in contrast to unsupported faith. When we cross the street we don't take it on faith that no cars are coming. We open our eyes and look, seeing what reality is. In every aspect of life, open your eyes and look at the evidence. Look.

We are naturalists, believing that everything that exists is within the cosmos as a working hypothesis. This seems, given the evidence, to be the best way to order our lives. We appear to have been born into a meaningless universe, but we are the meaning makers. Look into a child's eyes and tell me there is no meaning. Marvel at the rising sun, the cathedral of trees in an old forest, the redemptive power of love in times of strife, or a painting by Rembrandt; listen to a Bach fugue; or smell the warm earth in spring and you will find meaning. Because that is who we are—meaning makers.

Religion can engender feelings of awe and reverence, but we Humanists find emotional exhilaration in a life in the here and now: rich, full and immediate to our senses. Our consciousness is a product of our brain's activity. That means that when we die, our personality dies with the brain. If we live on, it is in our good deeds and the memories we leave. All this makes living so much more important, making our doing good here and now, with no heavenly reward or damnation, so pressing. It makes the demands of justice so much more pressing because if justice is to be done, we are the only ones to do it.

Some have claimed that without God or religion we become valueless nihilists. For us, in fact, it is just the opposite. Humanism really is an ethical way of looking at life without the supernatural. We act for good because it is in our rational self-interest and because we have a natural sense of empathy. We are hardwired for morality from a long evolutionary process because the survival of groups and individuals in them depended on it. As in all segments of society, some indeed never feel empathy for others, but most of us empathize with one another's pain and suffering. We desire a society that works toward the welfare of all and to minimize suffering.

Being a Humanist means taking responsibility for what you believe, what is really important, and how to live your life. It takes courage: courage to stand up to societal and family pressures we all feel; courage to think for yourself; and courage to find answers that stand up to reason and experience and not fall back on the simple answers that people are all too willing to give you. It means building a nontheistic life stance and a world view that many others already have chosen. If you want further information, you can find a copy of *Humanist Aspirations, the Humanist Manifesto III*, in Appendix I. Remember, though, that as a consensus document this is by no means the final word. Humanism is an evolving tradition. We Humanists never feel we have the final truth, as truth is never sealed. We have learned much through the years and will continue to learn more in the future.

The International Humanist and Ethical Union (IHEU) has defined Humanism in its Minimum Statement on Humanism:

"Humanism is a democratic and ethical life stance that affirms that human beings have the right and responsibility to give meaning and shape to their own lives. Humanism stands for the building of a more humane society through an ethics based on human and other natural values in a spirit of reason and free inquiry through human capabilities. Humanism is not theistic, and it does not accept supernatural views of reality."

Humanism considers the welfare of the natural world, rather than the welfare of a supposed God or gods, to be of paramount importance. If you have had religious doubts or are already a nonbeliever, then we may have some support for you. In this book I will flesh out more details about this evolving tradition, this naturalistic life stance, with its rich history and foundations.

2

Humanism in More Depth

I will attempt in this chapter to begin working on a deeper understanding of Humanism. There are many paths to Humanism. Some of us were raised in secular families or communities and want to plumb the depths of what the tradition holds for us. Some of us come out of liberal religious traditions, but find we desire the next level of authenticity. Some of us come out of more conservative religious backgrounds and have a tough time extracting ourselves from a totalizing and controlling culture. Some women, LGBT people and blacks come to Humanism from the realization that religion has traditionally been a tool of power and control over them. Regardless of your path, we all have to deal with the discrimination against nontheists that pervades our culture.

A study in 2011 in the *Journal of Personal and Social Psychology* found that atheists are some of the most distrusted members of society, ranking worse than murderers and rapists. We have a lot of work to do to refute this prejudice, but the data is certainly on our side. Studies have found that atheists have some of the lowest divorce rates, teen pregnancy rates, and rates of incarceration.

Rejection by families is one of the more heartbreaking results of this discrimination. Family members may react emotionally because they feel threatened when their most cherished beliefs and values, the overarching meaning in their lives, are challenged. We can make fun of them or get angry at their ignorance and closed-mindedness. Another way to see the situation, though, is to understand that they are reacting out of fear. Humanism can be a direct threat to what religious believers hold dear and what sustains them.

There is no right answer for how to deal with other people's emotional responses to religious beliefs. I am sure you are troubled by the fact that there is no polite way to tell a Muslim that he or she may have dedicated their life to an illusion. The same is true with whatever your own religious faith may be. Sometimes we have to stay in the closet. Sometimes we have to ask for understanding and respect. Sometimes all we can do is be kind, try to be a good person and wait for acceptance. Sometimes we need to accept that certain people will not accept us, maintain our own dignity and respect, and let it go.

All of us, at times, will compromise and silence ourselves to keep the peace and avoid rejection. It's toughest to be rejected by your parents, though. We may stay with our parents' religion because the risk of losing their love seems too great for most of us.

To religion's credit, it can provide a sense of community. The group that believes together stays together. Religion provides simple answers for how to live our life, where we came from, how to handle death, and how to find meaning in all of it. It can comfort us in our wounded moments. It can make the world "understandable." There is no question that these attributes can be of practical value for many.

On the other hand, a tradition of free thought asks us not to accept easy answers. It asks us to reject dogma, superstition, appeals to authority, special "revelation," coercive culture, and anything else that inhibits free thought. It rejects these not just because they do not lead to the truth, but because they are, in and of themselves, damaging to the human spirit and intellect. These methods likewise are rejected because they are easily used for power and control over those who are easily manipulated. Ultimately, people's dignity and freedom is denied when these methods are employed.

When I stopped believing, like most "come-outer" atheists, I was ready to do battle with anyone on matters of religion. I rationally brutalized my opponents, smug and confident of my reasoning. Still, when I went home, I felt a little dirty knowing that I had arrogantly humiliated my opponents. I knew that was not the right thing to do. More important, I knew I had not won over hearts with my rude methods. People judge your philosophy in a matter of seconds, not by rational arguments, but by your treatment of them. Ralph Waldo Emerson observed, "What you are stands over you the while, and thunders so that I cannot hear what you say to the contrary." I still struggle to learn that warning.

Something else concerned me. While I made fun of religion's grounding on a manmade book, authoritarian control, or faith based on personal revelation, I began to see that I myself had as little understanding about how to answer life's big questions. Embarrassment over my own hypocrisy drove me to pursue a lifelong search for what is true and how we should conduct ourselves. Just like religion, it's not easy to get beyond some of the shallow secular answers such as "Just be good." Those can be just as vapid as "Just believe in the Bible." Today, in relativist/postmodern times, it is even more difficult to find foundations because the answers are not simple. The answers I have found are many times layered, nuanced, interactive, and strikingly ambiguous. This book is an attempt to go beyond a primer on Humanism, and look at deeper questions of our grounding, the fundamental basis for our beliefs and whole world view. Think of this as a starter book for many of these ideas and I urge you look deeper at areas that may interest you.

I needed something to replace my lost beliefs in God. I eventually found satisfactory answers to most of my questions, but the quest continues. In recent years, when debating the religious, I always speak of a positive Humanism. I just ignore all the arguments about the Bible and God. When I do this, my religious opponents become befuddled; they are now on my turf and talking about my life stance, not theirs.

I use a functional definition of words when describing my position,. This means if a word works, I use it. Depending on the audience, I may identify myself as a naturalist, secularist, nontheist, atheist, rationalist, or such. I generally may start saying I am an atheist, but immediately add that I prefer to call myself a Humanist. Humanism best defines who I am and what I aspire to.

As a "come-outer," I arrogantly thought that the one truth, that there was no God, was all I needed. Humanism, by contrast, speaks to my whole secular life stance:

my world view, which is all about seeking the good life and good society.

Many who come out of religion go through the angry "come-outer" stage before moving on to a more reflective, encompassing Humanism. During that stage, we must let people vent and try to turn that energy toward a more productive activism. It is understandable that as a marginalized, oppressed segment of society, we will attract those whose frustrations may boil over.

A deep Humanism digs down below the surface of our nontheism into the foundation of our philosophy. It asks the big questions of life and is never satisfied with simplistic answers. It looks inward as well as outward, asking if we have our own house in order before marching off to do battle with oppressive forces.

Humanism's early founders placed a lot more emphasis on individual character than we do today. They knew that self-righteously proclaiming errors they had found in the Bible and the irrationality of belief in God, and railing against church-state entanglements, are only part of our duties. Duty requires that we do our best to dig deep in our Humanist garden and into our own lives to find what the good secular life entails. We have rightly moved in recent years to be more activist, but I hope we never forget to hold the mirror up to our lives, our own truths, our own meanings, and our own actions, and to reflect on the best of who we aspire to be.

3

What is Religion?

Imagine that we are sitting around a campfire with our family several thousand years ago after a long day's hunt. The endless expanse of stars above us speaks of our universe's unfathomable size, while the hot embers speak of life's unknown, enigmatic aspects. A young boy looks admiringly to his father, who has taught him since birth all he needs to know to survive in their harsh, hostile environment. Questions fill his young mind. In quick succession he asks, "What happens when we die? Where did we come from? Where did the world come from? Why are the woods scary? What are the stars? Why should I be good? Why do bad things happen?"

The father answers the best he can by telling the stories he heard from his father, what his own experience has told him, and what he imagines to be true. He even knowingly makes up answers to some questions. He might admit not knowing, but children are not easily dissuaded from asking a father who they believe knows everything else about life and the world.

I imagine this scene played out thousands of times in many lands over tens of thousands of years. There appears to be many reasons for the religious impulse, but certainly one of the most important is to be able to answer the deepest questions of life. The Harvard neurologist Michael Gazzaniga postulates an area in the brain's left hemisphere that he calls the "interpreter." Its function, he suggests, is to make sense of what we experience. It provides a narrative, an interpretive story, that may be part of what drives people to create and treasure religious stories. In prehistory, these stories were the best answers we could give.

The Old Testament, for example, is a collection of Bronze Age stories from one particular pre-scientific Middle Eastern tribe. Let's examine more of why the religious impulse is found in all cultures and carries such a profound impact in people's lives.

Just a cursory examination of religions such as Daoism, Islam, animism, Evangelical Christianity, ancient Greek paganism or intellectual Unitarian Universalism shows an incredible breadth of beliefs and practices. Examination of religion's various definitions is crucial as we go forward. Plato saw definitions as fixed and bounded, which we know is just not true. We will find the definition of religion can be quite flexible. If you engage in black and white thinking regarding definitions, you will be at a loss to understand religion's complexity. The standard dictionary definition is, "The service and worship of God or the supernatural." This is the definition that many people apply in daily use; hence, for most of us, the focus of religion generally centers on the supernatural.

Most scholars cast the net much wider. For example, Wilfred Cantwell Smith, the Harvard professor of comparative religions, saw religion as expressing, when everything is said and done, what we can ultimately have faith in. Faith, in this sense, means what we finally rely or trust upon. Paul Tillich, the Christian theologian, casts the net even wider and sees religion as that for which we have "ultimate concern."

Studying various cultures, many sociologists and anthropologists have found there is more to religion than just belief systems. The practice of religion in many cases was found to be more important in people's lives than its ideological aspects. Ritual, such as ceremonies for birth, marriage and death; setting up moral codes and taboos; the political power of priests and shamans; and, most important, religious community seemed more important than actual religious belief.

Anthropologists and sociologists introduced us to the idea that religion has both ideological and functional aspects. All of us know of Catholics, for example, who go to mass infrequently but love the ritual, and find religion marginally the basis for their beliefs about the world. They practice birth control, discount the pope's infallibility, and don't really believe in miracles. Such people find more importance in the Saturday night dance at church than in the Sunday morning service. Thus, to really understand what is going on in religion, we have to look through many lenses.

The field of study known as evolutionary psychology has helped us understand in recent years how a variety of religious impulses are evolutionarily successful adaptations for group cohesion and survival. Much debate continues as to whether these impulses are selected at the group level or are merely a result of a variety of other successful adaptations. Regardless, there seem to be cross-cultural and cross-generational genetic drives toward religious practices and beliefs. The origin of the word "religion" in Latin is *religio*, meaning "to bind together." That name seems to match our scientific understanding, so far, of how religion primarily functions.

The study of language is useful for our understanding of the word religion. The philosopher Ludwig Wittgenstein found that some words such as "beauty" and "love" don't have exact definitions. The term "family traits" is a metaphor that means a group of characteristics that seem to have some connection, but none of which is entirely definitive in describing a word. The term "family traits" comes from how people in certain families may have distinctive hair, nose, feet or posture, even if all these traits are not found in everyone in the family. Likewise, religion is one of those "fuzzy" words that are hard to pin down, with no exact definition, but can be seen to have a number of "family traits."

Rem Edwards, a philosopher of religion, illustrates how various modes of life we might call religion can be examined by a family trait model in the following table, which has been somewhat modified from his original concept:

SELECTED FAMILY TRAITS OF SOME SYSTEMS WORLD VIEWS

Excerpt Modifed from "Reason in Religion" by Rem Edwords (1980)

FAMILY MEMBERS

FAMILY TRAITS	CHRISTIANITY, JUDAISM, ISLAM	VENDATA HINDU PANTHEISM	EARLY THERAVADIC BUDDHISM	EARLY GREEK OLYMPIAN POLYTHEISM	COMMUNISM	HUMANISM	SPINOZISTIC PANTHEISM	SUCCESS, WEALTH, GOLF, FISHING
Belief in a supernatural intelligent being	P	A?	A	A	A	A	A	A
Belief in a supernatural intelligent being or beings	P	P	A	P	A	A	A?	A
Complex world view interpreting the significance of human life	P	P	P	P	P	P	P	A
Belief in experience after death	P	P	P	P?	A	A	A	A
Moral code	P	P	P	A	P	P	A	A
Belief that the moral code is santioned by a superior intelligent being or beings	P	P	A	A	A	A	A	A
An account of the nature of, origin of, and cure of evil	P	P	P	P?	P	P	P	A
Theodicy	P	P?	A	A	A	A	A	A
Prayer and ritual	P	P	P	P	P?	A	A?	A
Sacred objects or places	P	P	P	P	P	A	A	A?
Revealed truths	P	P	P?	P	A	A	A	A
Religious expeiience- awe, mysticalexperience, revelations	P	P	P	P	A	A	A	A
Deep, intense concern	P	P	P	P	P	P	P	P
Institutionalized social sharing of some of the traits above	P	A?	P	P	P	A?	A?	A?

Note that none of the traits are found in all of the family members except for Tillich's "deep concern." For my taste, Tillich's definition, while exploring an important feature of religion, casts too wide a net for our general concept of religion. To take one example, golf certainly does not seem to be a strong enough candidate to fit into our common perceptions of religion despite some people's devotion to it. One starts to question those families that seem to be in a "gray" area. That is, they have strong functional traits such as Theravada Buddhism or some Confucianism, but do not believe in a supernatural. Some say these are great world religions and some say not, depending on one's definition of religion. The word religion is a great example of the indeterminacy of some aspects of language and of life itself. We seek to put all things in nice order, with sharp distinctions and categories, but the world speaks to us ambiguously, requiring nuance, indeterminate boundaries, and metaphor. Too many times we try to impose order and exact definitions when there are none.

When we come to the issue of whether Humanism is a religion, there has been some controversy. In looking at the "family traits" of religion, some Humanists declare that one must draw the line somewhere, and that line should be the commonly held belief that religion centers around faith-based belief and devotion to the supernatural. Others point out that some Humanists, indeed all humans to some extent, use the functional aspects of religion.

Some Humanists call themselves religious, saying we should not throw out the baby with the bathwater but should keep those functional elements of religion that are useful. Ethical Culturalists, Humanistic Jews, nontheistic Friends, as well as some Unitarian Universalists and some

local atheist/Humanist chapters, try to develop supportive Humanistic communities that educate the children,
celebrate life passages, and develop rituals. Even among
Humanists, there is wide disagreement as to whether to
call themselves religious or not. Most do not, keeping in
mind that many Humanists find their lives work quite
well without being part of a specific Humanist community.
Instead, these people consider themselves better imbedded in the pluralistic community at large, as in much of
Europe.

So, is Humanism a religion or not? This is not just a
rhetorical question, but one of serious legal consequences
regarding the separation of church and state. Recently a
court case involving a prisoner seeking to start a humanist
group was decided in his favor as a "religious" right in
American Humanist Association v. United States. Evangelicals want to claim that Humanism is a religion that has
infiltrated and is destroying our schools. They argue that
evolution is a religious doctrine just as much as creationism
is, even though nothing could be farther from the truth.
Whether Humanism is defined as a religion depends on
the type of definition used. This isn't evading the answer.
If one asks if Humanism can perform some of religion's
functional qualities, the answer is yes: sometimes, but not
always. If one asks if it includes faith in a transcendental,
supernatural power, the answer is no.

The Merriam-Webster dictionary's first definition of
religion—"The service and worship of God or the supernatural"—is a good, practical, everyday definition that
most people use. Most people other than some religious
scholars, that is. Humanism should not be considered a
religion in common everyday language, as it is not su-

pernaturally based and is not faith based. The American Humanist Association acknowledges the reality that some people consider their particular form of Humanism to be religious in nature, which is different. Legally, it is settled law that some forms of Humanism and atheism can be seen as religious as well, e.g. when it comes to prisoners' "religious" rights. So it is best to acknowledge the pluralism of language in our movement and not get hung up on words.

John Dewey envisioned that it would be best to have our culture turn from theism to Humanism at a slow evolutionary rate rather than in a disruptive revolutionary process. In his book, *A Common Faith*, Dewey initially thought that one tool to accomplish this would be to use traditional religious words metaphorically. He tried to introduce a distinction between the noun "religion" and the adjective "religious," to be used during a transition period.

I make a somewhat similar distinction between religion and the set of religious impulses. Religious impulses should be seen not as just the expression of religion, but as the evolutionary, instinctual impulses that emanate from our core humanity. Some religions have sold the idea that these impulses are answered only by religion. I assert, to the contrary, that such impulses certainly "empower" religion, but they are our humanity speaking from a wide variety of primal drives.

Religion has no monopoly over the religious impulses of building like-minded intentional communities, practicing ethical teaching, or of trying to explain our origins, purposes and meanings. These are entirely human impulses seen in all cultures and all times, including modern secular cultures. Everyone has ultimate concerns. Everyone seeks an integrated worldview. Everyone has an emotional life. Everyone observes some sort of rituals.

Religion is different, though. Religion imagines unseen worlds and unseen gods as compelling narratives in our lives.

Dewey saw all our experiences involved in a "devotion to the ideal." The healthy person unifies and harmonizes all their experiences into a whole life in that devotion to the ideal.

Most of us search for an integrated worldview, of which there are two overarching great alternatives. One is based on whether one sees the world based on the evidence and naturalistically: that this world is all there is. The other one looks at the world with ungrounded faith and sees supernatural forces and worlds. Within each of these two great categories are countless other worldviews.

Most Humanists prefer to see their chosen path, their integrated worldview, as an evolving tradition, a philosophy, or a progressive life stance. For some, even these seem too rigidly doctrinaire. They prefer to see Humanism as more of a set of attitudes or approaches to the world.

The legal issues in the United States go back to the nation's founders. Most of the framers of the Constitution were Deists and followers of the Enlightenment philosophers. A Deist is one who believes a God created the world, but does not interfere afterwards or intervene in the affairs of humans. Many Deists believe that reason is the best tool to gain insights into the mechanisms of the world. Our founding fathers sought to create a government based on reason and human rights.

Thomas Jefferson told the Baptists of Danbury, Connecticut that the founding fathers wanted to build "a wall of separation" between church and state. To the founding fathers, religion meant faith-based belief in the supernatural and the institutions that foster that belief. They knew the horror of centuries of religious wars in Europe and wanted no part of it. The new government was to be secularly based and the process to be used in performing government functions was to be rational, in a democratic republic.

I prefer to use no adjectives in describing my Humanism: it is neither religious, ethical, nor secular. I have travelled widely in secular circles and have found little difference between all the different "styles." No matter how seculars describe themselves, be it Humanist, atheist, freethinker, etc., most agree on 95 percent of all beliefs and, more important, on values. Quibbling about our style, whether focused more on reason or experience, more communitarian or solitary, more anti-religion or more tolerant of religion, is fruitless. We all gravitate toward some style or emphasis that may fit us better than others, or we may even change our own style from day to day.

I want to explore Humanism from a positive standpoint, but it seems that I must deal with the issue, if only briefly, about the arguments for God's existence before moving on. Plenty of good books debunk religion. There are essentially two primary arguments given for belief in God, based on either reason or personal revelation. Within the arguments based on reason there are three primary arguments that were given full bloom in the writings of St. Thomas Aquinas and St. Anselm.

The three primary rational arguments generally given are these.

The ontological argument: Anselm of Canterbury, around the year 1078, defined God as "... that than which nothing greater can be conceived." He suggested that, if the greatest possible being exists in the mind, it must also exist in reality. The absurdity of this argument is that since I can conceive of unicorns and fairies they must exist as well. Conceivably anything that we can think of actually exists in reality. This is nonsense and just a result of Plato's ideas of immutable "forms."

The cosmological argument: Thomas Aquinas, who lived between 1225 and 1274, was a theologian in Medieval Europe. He modified arguments he found in his reading of Aristotle and Avicenna into his version of the cosmological argument. The argument is that the universe must have been caused by something that was itself uncaused, which must be God. Whatever begins to exist has a cause. The universe began to exist; therefore, the universe had a cause. The argument that everything has a creator begs the question: who then created God? It is a circular argument.

More recently, Christian apologists such as William Lane Craig have used a variant on the cosmological argument borrowed from Islamic theorists. The Kalam cosmological argument states that the first cause premise is supported by intuition and experience. He asserted that it is "intuitively obvious," based on the "metaphysical intuition that something cannot come into being from nothing."

The counter-argument is that we know scientifically that everything need not have a cause. For example, every time an atom decays it is a spontaneous process, from what we know, dictated only by the probabilities of quantum mechanics. Look at a luminescent watch dial that uses Radium 226 with a half-life of 1,600 years, which spontaneously gives off an alpha particle and turns into Radon 222. In accordance with quantum theory we can never know which atom will actually decay. Many times our intuitions are wrong, even with a common sense principle such as causation.

The teleological argument, also known as the argument from design: this is the most popular of the theist's arguments, which asks how such an intricate, complex world could come about without a creator. William Paley, an English clergyman and philosopher, in 1692 gave the example of a watch found on the ground, where we would automatically assume someone had created it.

This argument is intuitively compelling in the absence of scientific knowledge. This analogy is a false one, though, as a watch is known to be a human-made object whereas the universe's origin is unknown. Moreover, we can ask who created the watchmaker? It is a circular argument. Science continues its march to explain the world better and better; the more we know, the more the universe appears to be a bottom-up world. By that I mean the universe is inherently self-organizing and self-creating. Humans are creatures who order things and build patterns. The tendency to see order was an adaptation of some survival value, but sometimes we think we see patterns and order that are not there.

The emergence of complexity is an everyday natural occurrence in the formation of snowflakes, the fractal patterns of tree leaves, and the complex evolution of humans by natural selection. We like to think of intelligent causation, when many times natural processes are all that is. The designer we infer from complexity is really the natural result of the self-organizing of smaller units.

A more substantive question is what is known as the "fine tuning argument." This argument points out that several universal, fundamental physical constants must fall within a very narrow range to allow life in the universe, and that if any one of them were only slightly different, the universe would have been unlikely to be produce matter, the earth, or certainly carbon-based life.

Many critics of this argument point out that it is anthropomorphic: that it comes from a human-centered viewpoint. Humans are adapted to our particular universe through the process of evolution, rather than the universe having been adapted to humans. If we didn't have this exact universe, we would not be here analyzing it. We, as we are now, just wouldn't exist in any other universe to be talking about it. There may be billions of other universes in the cosmos where life did not emerge. We may indeed be the only sentient beings in our universe. Another universe with different physical constants might have life with totally different chemistry, such as silicon based. We also know that the fundamental constants are interrelated in some way and maybe, in a theory of everything, none of them are totally independent.

There is also an implication that "If science can't explain it, then it must be God." This is the so-called "God of the gaps." It doesn't logically follow that a lack of scientific knowledge about something means that only a supposition about God's existence will explain it.

The other main foundation for religion comes not from rational arguments, but from revelation. These revelations are both personal and subjective. Augustine of Hippo was one of the primary defenders of the knowledge of God by direct experience. Revelation finds its truths from ungrounded faith and personal experience, as God reveals himself to us by special, non-verifiable insights.

One may in fact have such experiences, but these experiences in and of themselves do not constitute facts or knowledge. I can imagine many things and have very vivid dreams, but that does not make them true. We know our beliefs are much colored by our social history and our own longings. We see what we want; talking to oneself is no proof of talking to God. Talking to an imaginary friend in the sky does not make it real.

Ultimately there is no certain proof that God or the supernatural does not exist, as one cannot prove a negative. What we can say with a high degree of certainty is that all supernatural beliefs are man-made. The evidence for this is overwhelming. Conversely, we see no credible evidence that gods exist, that miracles happen, that intercessory prayer works, that faith-based beliefs are effective, or that the world is anything but what is here and what we experience. There is little room to be totally noncommittal when looking at all the facts. One does not need certainty to stand firmly for a belief. Withholding judgment in the face of overwhelming evidence is not enlightenment, but neurosis.

The biggest indictment against the all-powerful, all-knowing, all-loving God of the Abrahamic religions is the problem of evil, known as the problem of theodicy.

Epicurus, a Greek philosopher from 341 to 270 BCE, gave
one of the best analyses of the problem when he said,
"Is God willing to prevent evil, but not able? Then he
is not omnipotent. Is he able, but not willing? Then he
is malevolent. Is he both able and willing? Then whence
cometh evil? Is he neither able nor willing? Then why
call him God?"

It just doesn't make sense. No amount of rationalization
can justify the countless deaths of innocents, the destruction
by natural forces like hurricanes, and the suffering that we
all endure, if we are under the control of an all-loving, all-
powerful God. Yes, this world contains incomprehensible
beauty, but also famine, war, hurricanes, painful childhood
diseases, rape, and the human appendix.

Of course there are other variants of the supernatural
other than an all-knowing, all-powerful god and we will
deal with these later in Chapter 11. But the Abrahamic,
controlling God is the dominant one. The Abrahamic
religions must answer the question of irresolvable incon-
sistencies in the model of God they present.

The arguments for or against religion could go on, but
essentially the Humanist argument deals with an analysis
of the evidence. There is just no good evidence for the
supernatural and a lot of evidence that says it is a human
fabrication. We can never close the door on the possibility
of God, but all the evidence points to a comprehensive
naturalism. At the end of a lecture by the mathematician
and philosopher Bertrand Russell, an angry woman asked,
"And Lord Russell, what will you say when you stand in
front of the throne of God on judgment day?"

Russell replied: "I will say: 'I'm terribly sorry, but you
didn't give us enough evidence.'"

Later, we will consider religion and religious impulses in more depth.

4

A Little History

Like a large old oak, our Humanist roots run deep. Ancient voices point us toward our highest ideals. We listened to those voices that urged us toward not the easy path, but a path of courageous integrity, the best of what we know, and the best that we can be. Our tradition has constantly pushed forward, sometimes bumbling down false paths, but, in the end, achieving real breakthroughs. It has eventually brought us to the place where we find ourselves today. Ours is still an evolving story, still incomplete, yet with significant advances. If we are to describe a deep Humanism, history can show us how the best ideas emerged and what has greater meaning and truth. Each piece added a little to our overall understanding of what promotes human welfare. History records our growing collective wisdom; we call it civilization. What follows is a history of some key turning points that led to the Humanism we have today.

Something happened concurrently in several areas of the world between 800 and 200 BCE, an explosion of new, but somewhat similar, ideas developed in what is called the Axial age. Before this, religion offered a partial remedy to the constant fear of famine, disease, and war. As populations increased, people placed more and more control in the hands of religious and political leaders. Some challenged this conformity to the traditional ideas and practices. It was during the Axial age that many more structured religions emerged, but also many ideas that contested them.

In India, Siddhartha Gautama, best known as the Buddha, developed a nontheistic philosophy of life that addressed suffering using real human tools. His eight-fold path of right view, intention, speech, action, livelihood, effort, mindfulness and concentration gave people guides to attaining a noble and virtuous life. In China, Lao-Tzu, the founder of Taoism, and Confucius, the founder of Confucianism, both offered common-sense, poetic wisdom, seeing ourselves as being an integral part of a natural world and dealing with practical human and social problems.

In the West, a culture developed in ancient Greece and in particular in the city-state of Athens in the time of Pericles that allowed people to start thinking and questioning just about everything that heretofore had been taboo. Solon and Pisistratus led the way toward democracy. The Athenians were some of the first recorded people to question what or who ran human lives. Were people under control of the gods or a predestined fate? Using critical intelligence, they saw that people largely controlled their own fates. Responsibility was directed back to the individual. While the Athenian philosophers were not what we would call Humanists in today's terms, due to such things as their subjugation of women, condoning of slavery and the like, they did start a tradition of using open-minded critical intelligence in which human responsibility is encouraged. Still, there is evidence that women did contribute to the intellectual development of the Periclean period.

Socrates famously said, "The unexamined life is not worth living for a human being." This may not be completely true for gaining the good life, but the idea of examining ourselves and the world around us is central to Humanist life.

The ancient Greeks gave so much to us. The Greek legend of Prometheus can serve as a metaphor for self-empowerment, where Prometheus supposedly stole the fire of the gods. In a sense, the Greeks asked us to take the fire of disciplined, open-minded free thinking, and use it to enlighten what otherwise was a dark and mysterious world. Protagoras stated that "Man is the measure of all things," not from an arrogance about the human condition, but to warn us not to judge anything except in the light of our own human subjectivity.

When we discuss our values, we are always bound by our own flawed perceptions and needs. Socrates taught us to use reason and critical thinking and to develop good character. He championed the wisdom of "Know Thyself," which was carved in the forecourt of the Temple of Apollo at Delphi. Aristotle taught us how to use logic and experience while developing personal character as a way to the good life.

In Rome, the Stoics expanded the Greeks' philosophical legacy. The Roman Emperor Marcus Aurelius wrote in his *Meditations* around 170 to 180 CE, "Live a good life. If there are gods and they are just, then they will not care how devout you have been, but will welcome you based on the virtues you have lived by. If there are gods, but unjust, then you should not want to worship them. If there are no gods, then you will be gone, but will have lived a noble life that will live on in the memories of your loved ones." Today, this is an important part of the Humanist outlook. We look at what we actually do rather than adhering to some abstract secular or religious doctrine. Deed, not creed, is our motto.

Three great world religions, Judaism, Christianity, and Islam, emerged from the Middle East. All these Abrahamic religious traditions tended to be absolutist, putting their focus on the supernatural with faith or authority as a guide. Contrast this to the great tradition arising out of the city of Athens that puts the locus of control and meaning in our hands, without absolute certainty. Jerusalem certainly was the focus for Judaism and Christianity, and important to Islam, too. These two cities gave rise to two very different foundations for our living that extends even to the present.

Keeping the intellectual fire alive outside of Athens proved difficult. Hypatia, the librarian of Alexandria, saw the value of these early philosophical texts. She died trying to protect them as Christians burned this cultural treasure. This quotation has been ascribed to her, but it may not be hers: "Fable should be taught as fable, myth as myth, and miracles as poetic fancies. To teach superstitions as truth is horrifying. The mind of a child accepts them and only through great pain, perhaps tragedy, can the child be relieved of them. Men will fight for superstition as quickly as for the living truth—even more so, since a superstition is intangible, you can't get at it to refute it, but truth is a point of view, and so is changeable."

Christianity began with many sects and beliefs. Two major early divisions were between the followers of Arius and of Athanasius. Arius and his followers thought Jesus was divine, but was not a god on the Father's level, whereas the followers of Athanasius believed in three gods in one God. The controversy reached a head when the Emperor Constantine called an assembly of bishops around 325. That First Council of Nicaea codified the original Nicene Creed and condemned Arius. Dissent within early Christianity was normal, but the church exerted greater and greater control after Constantine's conversion to an originally minor orthodox form of Christianity. Theocracy dimmed the light of reason and stifled dissent throughout much of Europe for hundreds of years. We are lucky that scattered pockets of civilization preserved and cultivated some of the Greco-Roman era's accomplishments.

Misogyny, always a problem, was given righteous authority by the church. Clement of Alexandria, a Christian theologian from around 150 to 215, wrote, "Every woman should be filled with shame by the thought that she is a woman." Martin Luther, in his *Works*, wrote, "The word and works of God is quite clear, that women were made either to be wives or prostitutes."

Pope Urban II instituted the ban on marriage of priests and bishops to prevent their property going to their heirs rather than the church, though he allowed priests and bishops to pay "sex taxes" and keep mistresses. He also launched the Crusades, which became a genocide, not just of Muslims, but of Christians as well.

Martin Luther showed his sentiments when he said, "Reason is a whore, the greatest enemy that faith has."

Luckily, during the Dark Ages, some Islamic scholars and others throughout Europe had protected some of the early Greek and Roman texts. As these texts became known throughout Europe, some Christian scholars embraced their ideas and melded them into religious thinking. Some scholars began emphasizing the human condition rather than the hereafter. In particular, the so-called Italian Renaissance Humanists such as Petrarch, Poggio Bracciolini, and Coluccio Salutati collected and studied the early Greek and Roman texts. Petrarch was even named the "Father of Humanism." Simultaneously work was being done in Spain, France, the Netherlands, and Germany. Scholars in these places embraced a study of what we now call the humanities. Slowly the focus shifted away from religious and biblical-based sources, undermining the tradition of Jerusalem, to the Athenian tradition that continues to this day.

The invention of the moveable type printing press by Johannes Gutenberg in 1439 allowed each person to have access to the Bible. Before that, the only people who could own, read and interpret the Bible were the priests and monks. With easy access to the Bible, people could read it for themselves. Each could become their own authority. Some found passages in the Bible they hadn't known about and began the Protestant Reformation, shifting authority and control from the church to the individual. Martin Luther declared that each individual was his or her authority in interpreting the Bible. Soon people were reading, thinking and sharing ideas and contesting blind authority to the Vatican. Bloody theological wars ensued, with each faction demanding loyalty. In one sense, we

are radical heirs to the Protestant Reformation, as this
revolution sought knowledge for oneself and freedom of
conscience over blind authority.

Eventually, thinkers such as Erasmus, Isaac Newton,
Pierre-Simon Laplace, and Galileo studied the predictable
regularities in nature and saw this as God's handiwork.
Many of the early scientists and philosophers were Deists who saw the world as a huge clockwork that God
had started up, but then left to its own devices. They
believed human reason was a divinely created tool for us
to uncover the regularities and mechanisms of an orderly
world designed by God.

Science started challenging biblical views when Nicolaus
Copernicus and Galileo contested the biblical and intuitive
view that the sun revolves around the earth. Only under
threat of torture and death did Galileo give a forced re-
traction of his views. After this renunciation, referring to
the supposed immovable earth, he was reported to have
muttered under his breath, "But it still moves!" It was
only in 1996, some 440 years later, that the Vatican issued
a statement acknowledging that Galileo had been right.

In the 1700s, the Enlightenment emerged, allowing the
full flowering of reason and science. The Enlightenment
philosophers challenged the authority of the monarchy.
In the process, they strengthened the idea, started during the Reformation, that individuals were capable of
discerning their own best interests and acting on them.
While ignorance, superstition and uncritical acceptance of
authority dominated the Middle Ages, the Enlightenment
would use literary analysis, reason and science as the best
methods for uncovering truth. In the process, Enlightenment thinkers challenged the suffocating domination of

religion. They saw rationality as a new guide that would result in unending progress. Humanity itself was perfectible, they asserted, and using rationality would lead to certain and necessary beliefs. Some skeptics, like David Hume, sought to temper enthusiasm for the newfound freedom and rational methods, looking more toward empirical evidence.

Even today, many Humanists speak of ourselves as being "Children of the Enlightenment," acknowledging our debt to their advances. Some of the primary figures were Nicolas de Condorcet, Mary Wollstonecraft, Voltaire, Rene Descartes, John Locke, Francis Bacon, Montesquieu, Thomas Hobbes, and Denis Diderot.

Denis Diderot provided the idea that, "Skepticism is the first step on the road to philosophy." Voltaire was more pointed in his attack on religion when he said, "Those who can make you believe absurdities can make you commit atrocities."

The romantic movement was a counter to the Enlightenment. The romantics saw direct experience, feeling, creativity, and passion as more important than reason in obtaining the good life; spontaneity and individualism were more important than discipline, order and control. Jean-Jacques Rousseau saw primitive, pre-scientific awareness as being truer to ourselves. Ludwig van Beethoven, Friedrich Schiller, Richard Wagner, William Wordsworth, Charles Dickens, Percy Shelley, and Johann Wolfgang von Goethe saw literature, art, music, and drama illuminating and advancing the human condition more than cold rationality. The Romantics sought non-rational methods to arouse awareness and passions that would improve civilization.

The founding of the United States represented a bold experiment in applying Enlightenment principles to government. Most of the founders did not want to repeat the 150 years of European religious wars or royal domination of political life. They wanted to give the new continent democracy, religious freedom, and separation of church and state.

Nearly all the founding fathers—George Washington, Thomas Jefferson, James Madison, James Monroe, Benjamin Franklin, Alexander Hamilton and Thomas Paine— were Deists. In fact, in 1776 only 17 percent of people even went to church. Of those, 70 percent of churchgoers were Congregationalists. Church membership built steadily over the years after that time, though, recently peaking around 54 percent of the U.S. population in 1994 in a study by Rodney Stark and Roger Finke.

Despite the founders' skepticism about conventional religion, it played a major role in the young republic's political disputes. Notoriously, the Bible was used to justify the practice of slavery. One study showed that 50 percent of the pro-slavery arguments before the Civil War referenced the Bible. One frequently cited verse is this passage from Exodus 21:7-11 (NLT): "When a man sells his daughter as a slave, she will not be freed at the end of six years as the men are. If she does not please the man who bought her, he may allow her to be bought back again. But he is not allowed to sell her to foreigners, since he is the one who broke the contract with her."

Recently, regarding slavery and present-day religious belief, the Humanist rap artist Greydon Square wrote in his *Myth Lyrics* raps:

Spoon fed this religion from the slave ship
They used faith to justify bringing slaves here
All the conducts and the rules in the good book
You swear by it, but failed to take a good look
You're completely sold
Just two centuries ago slave owners swore you didn't even
have a soul
Now you blindly defend a faith
That was used to plunder, pillage, and rape a whole entire race

Religion opposed, as it still often does, the full emancipation of women. Free-thinking women were at the
center of the fight starting in the nineteenth century. Eliza-
beth Cady Stanton said, "The Bible and the church have
been the greatest stumbling block in the way of women's
emancipation." Her famous rallying cry, "No Gods, No
Masters," was a first step towards women's liberation.

Women increasingly came to realize how religion was
used as the justification for male domination. The Seneca
Falls Convention, held in Seneca Falls, New York in 1848,
was the first women's rights convention. These first-wave
feminists knew all too well how patriarchy was justified,
citing Bible quotations such as: "Let your women keep
silence in the churches: for it is not permitted unto them
to speak; but they are commanded to be under obedience,
as also saith the law. And if they will learn anything, let
them ask their husbands at home: for it is a shame for
women to speak in the church." – I Corinthians 14:34-35.

After Abraham Lincoln's assassination, his law part-
ner and closest associate Thomas Herndon wrote in his
biography of Lincoln, "Mr. Lincoln was an infidel of the
radical type, sometimes bordering on atheism. . . . He

never mentioned the name of Jesus, except to scorn and
detest the idea of a miraculous conception. He did write
a little book on infidelity in 1835-6 and never recanted."
Lincoln's friends persuaded him to burn that book, correctly viewing it as a political death sentence. "He was an
out and out infidel, and about that there is no mistake,"
Herndon declared.

The interviewer Opie Read once asked Lincoln his
conception of God and he replied, "The same as my conception of nature."

Throughout these historic dramas, various people
stopped believing in God or gods, but people never had
an alternative overarching story to tell that was at once
naturalistic, reasonable, and coherent. Remember that
most of the philosophes in France were atheists, but had
no alternative story. Ralph Waldo Emerson was a liberal
Unitarian minister in the early part of the nineteenth century
who developed the concept of transcendentalism and of
the undefined "oversoul." His conception of the oversoul
was totally naturalistic. He never defined the oversoul,
for a good reason: there was no good story of our origins
at the time that he developed it. That was true, however,
only until Darwin's publication of *The Origin of Species* in
1859, which Emerson then embraced.

Darwin's concept of an ancient, self-organizing, evolutionary process melded with the geologist Charles Lyell's
evidence of an old earth. Together, these scientists gave
us a new story that was at once bold, compelling, wide-
ranging, scientific, and at odds with all the old faiths.
Those who doubted God's existence now had their own
Genesis story to tell.

The latter part of the nineteenth century saw the emergence of the Freethought movement, which rejected religion. Freethinkers hold that truth should be formed on the basis of logic, reason, and evidence, rather than authority or tradition. Freethought communities sprung up across the United States, but then rather quickly fell apart. The philosopher William Kingdon Clifford spoke for their position, saying, "It is wrong always, everywhere, and for anyone, to believe anything upon insufficient evidence." They saw religion as ultimately nonsense, overly powerful, and harmful.

The best known spokesperson for Freethought was Colonel Robert Ingersoll, "The Great Agnostic" as he was known. It was an age when public speakers were the rock stars of their age, attracting thousands to their lectures, and Robert Ingersoll was the most popular. He produced many wonderful quotations such as, "I admit that reason is a small and feeble flame, a flickering torch by stumblers carried in the starless night,—blown and flared by passion's storm—and yet, it is the only light. Extinguish that, and naught remains." One of his most famous statements of principle is included in Appendix 2. Ingersoll called for a "Religion of Humanity." The Freethought anti-religious tradition still influences much of Humanism today.

In the late nineteenth century, liberal religion faced a dilemma as to whether to embrace new scientific ideas or fall back to the old dogmas. Felix Adler in New York aspired to be a rabbi like his father before him, but after studying in Europe he concluded that the ideological aspects were not important in religion, and that the functional aspects of community and ethics were what mattered. He preached one sermon about these ideas in 1876 at his father's synagogue. It quickly became apparent that he would not succeed his father. He then founded the Ethical Culture movement. It has since has been on the leading edge of social reform and personal ethics, dominated by a naturalistic Humanist bent. Adler called for a reconstruction of the moral ideal.

The Ethical Culture movement put its humanism into social action, working in the immigrant slums of New York, Chicago and elsewhere and especially protecting children. The movement started the Legal Aid Society and helped found the National Association for the Advancement of Colored People and the American Civil Liberties Union.

In the later part of the nineteenth century, the use of the word "Humanism" was starting to evolve. The philosopher F. C. S. Schiller wrote a book called *Humanism* that was based on a kind of philosophical pragmatism, certainly not the kind of Humanism as we know it today. The meaning of the word Humanism began to evolve beyond the way it had been practiced by Renaissance Humanists.

Likewise during the late nineteenth century, the Unitarian movement began to focus on the use of reason in religion over blind faith. It promoted the ideal of freedom of thought and conscience, but still found itself in an internal debate regarding the new knowledge about religion and evolution. In particular, many Unitarian ministers in the Midwest embraced evolution, reason, and empirical science while rejecting theism. They even formed a nontheistic splinter group called the Western Conference that almost led to a schism amongst Unitarians over the theism/nontheism issue.

Two important Unitarian ministers, John Dietrich and Curtis Reece, embraced the new naturalistic way of thinking and found out they were both preaching the same nontheistic ethical message. In 1917 they mutually decided to call it Humanism, a term Dietrich had been using and was then being used rather broadly in intellectual circles. We owe them for popularizing the modern meaning of Humanism as an integrated, naturalistic, ethical whole life stance aimed at improving humanity and the earth.

John Dietrich professed a hardnosed and unapologetic Humanism. He gave a sermon called "The Folly of Half-Way Liberalism," in which he said he was "ashamed . . . of the complacency . . . from a reactionary leadership of those who assume to wear the mantle of religious liberalism, yet who—either through a caution borne of worldly ambitions, or through a mind enfeebled by the lack of intellectual discipline, or through a soul too weak to bear the rigors of an open sea—persist in giving comfort to all those forces of reaction that have bound their souls in the horrible shackles of fear and darkness." It is amazing, in reading his *Ten Sermons*, how similar were the attacks he faced one hundred years ago from both fundamentalists and "half-way" liberals, as he called them.

Dietrich and like-minded ministers were trying in many ways to integrate the Enlightenment and Romantic movements. They realized that all the pieces of a naturalistic world view were starting to come together. They were trying to unify that thought into a cohesive whole, using the functional aspects of religious community with none of the supernaturalism. More and more ministers joined in this movement, along with a number of philosophers. As they battled for acceptance, the term "Humanism" caught on as the unifying symbol of a modern, scientific, naturalistic, and integrated life philosophy within liberal religion and academia. Much of what we know as Humanism today grew from these pioneers. They were modernists, optimistic about the prospects for humanity.

Many Americans looked towards a future of progress led by science and technology. After centuries of war in Europe, war was looking like a thing of the past. Art, literature, and music were advancing our culture as well. Technology offered a utopian future that would advance humanity's prospects. The modernist outlook saw rationality as an unequivocal good. Humanity was viewed as essentially good and infinitely malleable, and cultural and political progress would take us to new heights. Modernism, as a child of the Enlightenment, saw the world as having knowable, universal, objective and absolute truths when reason was applied. Progress was an inevitable historical, rational, and scientific project. A better social order could be developed as we uncovered our common human nature and applied science to human problems. A technocratic kind of utopianism underlay this secular modernist vision.

John Dewey was one of the most important voices in the development of modern Humanism. Here is how he put it. "In sober fact, we are living at a stage in history which relatively speaking is so immature that . . . our science is technical rather than widely and deeply human. The philosophers of the seventeenth, eighteenth, and nineteenth century did an important work in promoting conditions which removed obstacles to the progress of physical and physiological science. There is now a supreme challenge, a supreme opportunity. If Galileo and his successors could look upon this gathering here today he would say, 'It is for you to do for the very life of man what we did for the physical and physiological conditions of that life. Discovery of these conditions was for us the immediate task that determined the end of our search. You possess the results of that search. It is for you to use them as means to carry forward the establishing of a more humane order of freedom, equity, and nobility. We accomplished the simpler and more technical part of the work. It is for you, possessors of a torch lit by our toil and sacrifice to undertake, with patient and courageous intelligence, a work which will hand on to your successors a torch that will illuminate a truly human world.'"

Many thought it was time to compile a summary of the Humanist worldview, especially because they were worried that civilization was breaking down. This was to be a summary of the best of what civilization knew at the time. In 1933, Unitarian ministers Raymond B. Bragg and Edwin H. Wilson, along with the philosopher Roy Wood Sellars, wrote a one-page document, the *Humanist Manifesto*. It was a consensus document, with not everyone who signed it in total agreement on every point. Due to the Depression, it was as much a political statement as a philosophical one. It reflects the times as any historical document does. We view the language today as sexist and it also has a socialist bent, which reflected the deep concern that capitalism's problems needed bold new solutions. Still, its simple and clear vision, in a single page, told our story well at the time.

The Great War and then the Great Depression challenged the 1930s generation's modernist hope that life was progressively getting better. Modernism's utopian vision was short-lived. The Dadaist art movement first denied any positive vision for art, but the Great War also brought political and cultural progress into question. The senseless slaughter vividly undermined the idea of the essential goodness and rationality of people. World War II, the Holocaust, and their 50 to 80 million deaths further challenged the notion that we were becoming more civilized. Western civilization seemingly stood on the brink of total collapse. The barbarism was overwhelming. Scratched into a wall at Auschwitz were the words, "If there is a God he will have to ask my forgiveness." Primo Levy, a survivor of the Holocaust, said, "There is Auschwitz so there cannot be God."

Between the two world wars, the Great Depression laid waste to dreams of an ordered, rational economy. Modernist utopian dreams dissolved in the struggle for daily economic survival in the United States and Europe. In Russia, meanwhile, the Stalinist purges that would eventually kill an estimated 30 to 50 million people were in full force, but became widely known in the West only around 1938. That an atheistic regime was capable of such atrocities further discredited many idealistic notions.

After the Second World War, Humanists changed the *Humanist Manifesto II* and *III* with the realization that progress was elusive at best. These updated documents recognized that we have the potential for both great good and great evil with only a thin veneer of civilization covering over a fairly barbaric nature. Our dreamy-eyed illusions about progressively perfectible humanity were buried in the ashes of the Holocaust.

European postmodernist Marxists explained the failure of Communism in Russia as the result of Enlightenment modernist ideas of rationality. How is that, you may ask? Theodore Adorno and Max Horkheimer, in their book *Dialectic of Enlightenment*, saw that the rise of National Socialism, state capitalism, and mass consumer culture were forms of mass of social domination resulting from an oppressive and totalizing rationality. Reason had become only a tool for power and control by powerful interests over the masses. All so-called "rational truths" came into question as mere rationalizations and mere cultural artifacts.

Postmodernism or continental philosophy, as it is sometimes known, ultimately saw all knowledge as a social construction and both the Enlightenment and Romantic movements as merely tools to rationalize power and control over others. You may not know anything about postmodernism, but you can hear it in everyday phrases like, "One belief is as good as another," "Who am I to judge?" and "It's all relative." It is the water we swim in. It breeds a nihilism of heart and mind.

Edwin Wilson went on and should be credited as the tireless promoter of Humanism, editing the *New Humanist* magazine, and, in 1941, helping to organize the American Humanist Association. This was the only organization at the time exclusively promoting secular advancement. The International Humanist and Ethical Union (IHEU) formed in 1952, linking people throughout the world with our secular life stance.

In the nineteen fifties and sixties, Humanism dominated the Unitarian Universalist Association. It became one of the fastest growing denominations in the United States, with a focus on nontheistic Humanism. Humanism was being mainstreamed, dominating in academia and liberal circles, while at the same time having to fight against conservatives during the McCarthy period. Still, it looked like Humanism might take over the general culture, especially after *Time* magazine put "Is God Dead?" on its April 8, 1966 cover.

Many considered religious fundamentalists to be mostly backwoods kooks and that secularism and Humanism were taking over our general culture. That was until Jerry Falwell and the Moral Majority became the vanguard of the conservative revolution in the late seventies. I met Falwell once and can attest that he was a savvy, brilliant leader who was seriously underestimated. Jerry Falwell's abilities taught me to not stereotype fundamentalists as stupid or ignorant. I then understood that ideology of any sort can distort even the brightest minds. Movement conservativism linked with the Religious Right today are now the biggest challenges to Humanism. Kurt Anderson in his book *Fantasyland* traces the American tendency towards magical thinking now dominating America back to the Puritans which was promoted by expanding religious fundamentalism. How things have changed.

It wasn't just postmodernism and resurgent religious fundamentalism that worked against Humanism and its principles during the twentieth century. A series of other developments also worked to undermine reason and science. Earlier, Bertrand Russell and Alfred Whitehead had worked for many years to prove that mathematics was a result of logic. As Russell wrote, it is the logicist's goal "to show that all pure mathematics follows from purely logical premises and uses only concepts definable in logical terms." They published the three-volume *Prinicipia Mathematica* in 1910, 1912, and 1913. That quest was undone by the criticisms of Russell's own student,

Ludwig Wittgenstein. Russell held that all propositions can be analyzed into simple symbols that refer to objects, whereas Wittgenstein denies that all meaning is ultimately referential. For Wittgenstein, the meaning of an expression is just its contribution to the sense. It is a highly complex linguistic argument that convinced Russell his quest was a fruitless one. Then Kurt Gödel developed his famous incompleteness theorem, which states that if a system is consistent, it cannot be complete. The consistency of the axioms on which the system depends cannot be proven within the system itself. No rational system can have all the answers. Any system of logic will always contain one true, but unprovable statement. In other words, no matter how hard we try to prove something it is never a complete argument. There is always something more. Bertrand Russell's quest to show all of mathematics as a result of logic could never be complete.

A whole neo-romantic revolution in popular culture added further assaults to reason and modernism and by implication to Enlightenment-based Humanism. The new age movement emerged as a mixture of gullible romantic and pseudoscientific beliefs. It morphed into an overblown utopian idealism about the potentialities of human nature. Culturally and intellectually it has credulously embraced every kind of magical thinking, including homeopathy, astrology, faith healing, energy fields, angels, ESP, Qigong, spiritualism, reincarnation and an infinite variety of other optimistic but irrational beliefs. Acceptance of these new-age notions increased two- to five-fold in twenty-five years. As the atheist author Susan Jacoby said, "This mindless tolerance, which places observable scientific facts, subject to proof, on the same level as unprovable supernatural fantasy, has played a major role in the resurgence of both anti-intellectualism and anti-rationalism."

The second-wave feminist revolution, led by mostly by Humanists such as Betty Friedan, Gloria Steinem, and Simone de Beauvoir, was a welcome advancement in equal rights and dignity. Some studies indicated that men's modes of thinking were tilted toward the rational while women were tilted toward the intuitional and the empathetic, towards caring and concern. The original studies concerning ethical orientation were led by the psychologist Carol Gilligan, and many others followed. Some have disputed these studies.

However, a disturbing trend was also occurring in academia during this time. Many feminists in academia embraced postmodernism, believing rationality is primarily a method for male dominance over woman. This undoubtedly occurs, but rationality was disparaged and not seen as an imperfect human tool available to both men and women for the betterment of all. Nevertheless, third-wave feminists have largely abandoned the postmodern relativism and embraced reason and science as tools for examining and challenging gender discrimination.

That evolution in feminist thought coincided with a number of other trends that once again began to advance Humanist values.

The internet revolution has contributed to the secular revolution since around 2004. Just as the Gutenberg press expanded knowledge of what was in the Bible, the internet allows many to see alternative viewpoints and data about all of religion. The "new atheists" Christopher Hitchens, Sam Harris, Daniel Dennett, and Richard Dawkins wrote hardnosed antitheist books that attacked religion and religious beliefs. Secular ideas and values have been rapidly advancing, especially among youth. But Humanism in all its fullness, the next step, is still not well known by the general public.

The secular landscape is rapidly changing today. The nonreligious and nontheists are now the fastest growing demographic segments in the US, even though the demographics show we are shrinking in the world due to the higher birthrates of thiests. Still, no one should become complacent with this trend, considering the lingering cultural disorientation of postmodernism and fundamentalism, even if in its death throes, still gripping our culture. A trend is a trend until it's not, and the future is still unwritten.

The recent political turn to the right is an unprecedented rejection of humanist values, but was presciently predicted in 2000 by Rabbi Sherwin Wine. He was a gay atheist rabbi, the founder of the Society for Humanistic Judaism, and possibly the wisest and most brilliant man I have ever known. "There are two visions of America. One precedes our founding fathers and finds its roots in the harshness of our Puritan past. It is very suspicious of freedom, uncomfortable with diversity, hostile to science, unfriendly to reason, contemptuous of personal autonomy. It sees America as a religious nation. It views patriotism as allegiance to God. It secretly adores coercion and conformity. Despite our constitution, despite the legacy of the Enlightenment, it appeals to millions of Americans and threatens our freedom.

"The other vision finds its roots in the spirit of our founding revolution and in the leaders of this nation who embraced the age of reason. It loves freedom, encourages diversity, embraces science and affirms the dignity and rights of every individual. It sees America as a moral nation, neither completely religious nor completely secular. It defines patriotism as love of country and of the people who make it strong. It defends all citizens against unjust coercion and irrational conformity.

"This second vision is our vision. It is the vision of a free society. We must be bold enough to proclaim it and strong enough to defend it against all its enemies."

It's been a rough ride from the early confidence of Humanist pioneers who were trying to stitch together the best of human thought. We have learned that pure rationality can be misused as a tool, merely confirming our hidden prejudices. We have learned there is no simple formula for living. We now understand that we should humbly accept the limitations of what we can accomplish towards the good life. We are challenged today by the resurgent anti-intellectualism of the religious right. Still, we are optimistic and like a rodeo rider: we have to dust ourselves off and ride the bucking bronco of life again and again. If Humanism has one hallmark, it is courage. It is far easier to accept the simple packaged nonsense of either religion or of a postmodern radical relativism.

We still find that reason, science and compassion are our best guides.

Humanism requires open-mindedness, intellectual discipline, an open heart, social responsibility, and the ability to deal with ambiguity. History has shown that we have no certain guide to follow, no grand narrative, no one certain way. If we are to progress in any sense, we need all the human tools to help us integrate our best strategies with courage, compassion, reason. All the while, we must continue loving this enchanting earth, our families, friends, and neighbors, and our own flawed, yet noble, humanity.

5

What are the Sources of Knowledge?

You've heard it all before. Fundamentalists—be they Christian, Muslim, Jew, Mormon, Baha'i, or Hindu—will tell you that there is only one way: their way. They will tell you there is only one authority for belief and that is their holy book, be it the Bible, Koran, Book of Mormon, the writings of Baha'u'llah or the Upanishads. You also hear from some Catholics that the final word for determining truth comes from their final authority, the pope. Some say their religious belief and fervor came about from a personal experience in which God spoke directly to them.

The secular can be just as dogmatic about their personal experiences. Some say they have strong intuitions that tell them directly what is true. Some say reason can give them absolute certainty and speak in certain terms of a truth that guides all actions in their lives.

Conversely, some have said our lives should instead be guided by rational principles. There are others who say we should guide our lives by the evidence. Others say by whatever seems to work.

In recent years we have heard from some called post-modernists that objective truth is an illusion and that reality is only each individual's perception. As we learned in the previous chapter on history, postmodernists tell us our versions of truth are mere social constructions and that no one truth or culture or religion is better than any other. Reason and science are Western tools for oppression and control, and are the basis for only one "story" out of many that are equally valid. Postmodernists tell us we should then live only in ironic, tolerant acceptance of our own story and others.

Are you confused? Is it any wonder that in the twenty-first century we find ourselves talking past each other? Is it any wonder that we find our culture in a balkanized war of values, beliefs, goals and understanding? Is it any wonder that we find people filled with doubt, uncertainty, and anxiety, and sometimes falling into cynicism and apathy, while others fall into dogmatic fundamentalist certainty? In 2016 the number-one new word was "post-truth." It's easy to see how, in these rough waters, many people will latch on to any life raft of belief. In Latin the phrase, *Mundis vult decepi* – "The people want to be deceived" tells us why people want to believe lies. My challenge to all this confusion is simple. Dare to know. There is an ethics of belief that requires us to believe responsibly. We will find that reason will ultimately triumph.

What we now want to determine, if it is even possible, is how to find the truth of things. What can we believe with confidence? Belief is easy. Determining knowledge is hard. Knowledge only comes after something convinces us of its truth and seems to tell us how the world really is. It goes back to Plato's definition that **knowledge is true, well-grounded belief.** But what do we mean by "well-grounded?" Traditionally, **truth is where a belief is in accord with reality.** The study of what we know and how we know it is called epistemology. We will deal with values in Chapter 7, but one of the traditional ways to order our thoughts is to separate the facts from our values. It a useful separation as long as we realize that the facts, the way things are, can (and should) influence our values, and vice versa. Our values can change how we view the facts, interpret them, and prioritize them.

Three major definitions of faith often get conflated and confused. We need to distinguish them:

a. Faith – Belief, reliance, or trust in something with evidence;

b. Faith – Belief, reliance, or trust in something in absence of evidence; and

c. Faith – Belief, reliance, or trust in something in spite of the evidence.

The last one is commonly referred to as religious faith or blind faith.

As a Humanist, I choose to believe in: (a) ideas that have evidence to support them; I will settle on a decision when I have to (b) in the absence of evidence; and I will reject ideas that are (c) not consistent with the evidence. For example, I believe and trust that evolution is true because of the preponderance of evidence for it. I refuse to believe or trust creationism because the evidence clearly refutes it. But I can trust that the future will be better than today without any evidence as it is helpful for me to think positively. Humanism stresses using *reason, which is the power of comprehending, inferring, or thinking, especially in orderly, rational ways.*

Let's cut to the chase. For Humanists, we find that reason and science, not blind religious faith, are the best, but not the only, way to develop knowledge about the world. It's really pretty simple: Humanists look to the evidence for belief. For some of you, that answer may be enough and you can stop reading this chapter now. What follows is an extended explanation that may be too much for some. If it is, I can certainly understand. This can be tough and confusing. We want to keep it simple, but not too simple. For others of you who want to explore a deeper conversation of what grounds our beliefs and our knowledge, read on.

Listed below are a few of the alternative ways that many people (not philosophers) generally say they both find and ground knowledge. We will examine each of them:

1. By authority
2. By direct experience
3. By revelation
4. By intuition/instinct
5. By rationalism
6. By science
7. By no way – postmodernism
8. By civilization
9. By whatever works

Let's examine each perspective in turn for its merits and problems.

Authority: If we go back to the prehistoric campfire scene: we will remember that the father gave his children the best information he could give, speaking as the authoritative figure in their lives. We might poke fun at his primitive answers, but must remember that was the best they had back then. Even today, most of us growing up rely on parents, sisters and brothers, teachers, and friends for our development. More recently, media, newspapers, radio, television, movies and the internet may serve as "authorities." We tend to grow up believing our parents' religious faith. Other studies show that children's peers and siblings have more influence than their parents on their eventual adult personalities and values.

There is no doubt we each need mentors to help us, and that they can exert a great influence over our beliefs. Still, we should question all so-called authority. If so-and-so is an authority, what gives that person the special track to knowledge? Catholic doctrine says the pope has ultimate authority of the church and knowledge because they interpret Jesus saying to Peter, "On this rock you shall build my church" as meaning the Catholic church is the one and only true church with Peter and his successors being in charge. The First Ecumenical Council of the Vatican of 1869–1870 codifed papal infallibility where the Pope is preserved from the possibility of error "when, in the exercise of his office as shepherd and teacher of all Christians, in virtue of his supreme apostolic authority, he defines a doctrine concerning faith or morals to be held by the whole Church." But that begs the question of how we know that is true? He can assert that he is the ultimate authority to interpret the Bible—if he interprets the Bible that way. This is what is known as a "circular argument."

While authorities and experts are valuable for all of us, especially in science and daily expertise, they cannot be used as an ultimate basis for knowledge.

Direct Experience: All of us have inner lives that are inaccessible to others. We have a rich internal conversation in our minds that cannot be seen or observed. We have conscious experiences that we try to share the best we can. But as we all know, the actual act of experiencing things, especially our emotions, remains opaque to others. No one can actually experience our pain, our hopes, our joys, and our dreams. We may have empathy with others' experience, but that falls short of the actual experience others feel. Many times, we Humanists focus on knowledge of the world's facts, but existential reality of our consciousness always stands before us. We are the universe looking at itself. We are the universe gaining consciousness.

Let's do a little existential experiment and say to yourself, "All of us are mortal." This is a perfectly logical statement that all of us rationally agree with. Now say to yourself, "I am going to die." Note that this draws an abstract, rational truth inward toward our own experience. Now take in this statement: "I am dying." A visceral awareness of our own death resonates in most of us in certain existential ways. That is why the philosopher Jean-Paul Sartre said existence precedes essence. The abstract essence of things is that all of us are mortal, but the subjective existential fact of our own deaths can lead to a variety of personal, experiential meanings.

Science has come a long way in understanding consciousness and emotions and capturing the biological processes that underlie them, but it cannot penetrate to how we actually feel. I know I love my wife as surely as I know anything. Maybe it is only an implanted feeling from an electrical probe in my brain; maybe my brain is in a vat. Nevertheless, I know the feeling of love I am having is real to me. I know what disgust feels like. I know what shame and the loss of freedom feel like. All these feelings may be some of the most important things I know, over and beyond the facts of the world. Consciousness is a nonreductive emergent property. Science cannot prove I love my wife or love justice, and yet they are central to everything I am.

Can our inner experiences be delusional? Of course, and we will discuss that in the next section. This is why we need other frames of reference to understand what goes on in our consciousness. For as we shall next see, our direct experience can lie to us. Still, our experiences in and of themselves are real as anything we know, and knowledge of our inner lives can come only from direct experience.

Revelation: Special revelation of the truth from direct experience has been claimed by many. The best-known example is Moses, but there are countless others from Mohammed and Joseph Smith to Adolf Hitler and President George W. Bush—who reportedly said God told him to attack Iraq—and any number of evangelists today. They all say the truth was revealed directly and personally to them. These are examples of religious and political leaders, but many ordinary people also say they have had experiences that gave them special knowledge. Some report that special methods allow them to achieve those revelations.

Some Native Americans say using peyote allows them visions of truth. Similarly, many who have taken LSD and other hallucinogenic drugs report "religious experiences." Zen monks report that after fasting and deep meditation the world as it is comes into view. The whirling dervishes report that during their spinning, they enter into union with God. So it is with other meditative sects such as followers of Transcendental Meditation. Some report that the truth was revealed to them in dreams. Many see truth in magical methodologies such as Tarot cards, astrology, reading "bones," therapeutic touch or palm reading.

In all these cases, a particular experience occurred that, according to the believers, gave them a compelling belief that God had talked to them. This belief was then transmitted to others who also held it to be true. In some cases there is good reason to believe the person may be trying to hoodwink us. For example, there is documentation that Joseph Smith, the founder of Mormonism, was involved with his family as a con man in his early years, working treasure-hunting scams. Many of these cons were based on stories of ancient tribes. In later years, Smith said the angel Moroni told him where to find golden tablets describing a story of the lost tribes of Israel settling in America. Later he was chosen the leader of the religion that allowed him many wives and gave him special revelation directly from God. He claimed that the golden tablets were later magically transported to heaven. In similar fashion, Mohammed reported that God talked to him through an angel, and told him he could have as many wives as he desired. One does not need to be a scholar of human motivation to have suspicions of these accounts' truthfulness.

Still, in many other instances, we have no reason to doubt the sincerity of the people telling similar stories. Many report that God spoke directly to them. You probably know of someone who claims they have had a personal religious experience with God. The crucial thing to remember here is that experiences, no matter how powerful and seemingly true, no matter how transformative to the person in shifting either their behavior or their ideas, constitute a knowledge only of the experience itself. They add nothing to our knowledge base other than that some people had a powerful and meaningful experience. William James, in his landmark book, *The Variety of Religious Experience*, provides a wonderful analysis of these experiences.

A competing theory suggests what has actually happened rather than God talking to us. We know that we humans make up things, and even hallucinate, especially under the effects of drugs, dreams, fasting, hypnosis, stimulus deprivation or stimulus overload. The mind is fragile and can easily be altered to imagine things, in particular those things we desire or already have been mulling over. Mystical experiences, while profoundly compelling, can tell us more about ourselves than anything else. When one says God spoke directly to them, how do we know the voice didn't come from the devil, or an alien, or as a schizophrenic I knew thought, from the CIA? The most obvious common-sense answer, based on both our scientific and personal experience, is that people were talking to themselves.

Intuition: At one time or another we have all had a sense while talking with someone that they are lying to us. We don't know exactly why, but it just feels like it.

Sometimes this is called intuitive knowledge. Intuition is an immediate sense of knowing something seemingly without reason or experience. We just seem to "know."

Intuition seems to be an inherent quality of the brain that evolution provided to be a quick guess about a situation. It appears to be borne of a subconscious process that integrates whatever knowledge we have and synthesizes a quick answer. In other words, a lot of reasoning is going on, just not at a conscious level. In some cases, the knowledge being used appears to be hard-wired into our brains in what we call instinct and is not easily accessible by direct consciousness.

Take the example of lying. We now know, through indirect scientific methods, that the brain is instinctually wired to detect very small muscle strains, twitches and forms that signal when a person is lying. There is a rational, subconscious process using evolutionary adapted skills, but we just aren't aware of the process. Many neurological studies confirm that most of our thinking is subconscious.

The life work of the psychologist Daniel Kahneman, winner of the Nobel Prize for Economics, centers on the idea that we have two modes of thinking, fast and slow. Type 1, or fast thinking, is the automatic mental process of intuition, perception, and memory. It helps us survive by creating a coherent pattern of beliefs that result in quick assessments and decisions. It tends to neglect ambiguity, and confirms our biases. Type 2, or slow thinking, involves more open-minded, rational, deliberate, and effortful thought.

Fast intuitive thinking is needed in most aspects of daily life. You don't survive a lion attack by taking time to analyze the situation. Your finely tuned instincts about a person lying are generally pretty good. Who really thinks carefully about opening a door in your own home? Still, acting on our inherent biases and instincts without deliberative confirmation leads to many errors. Kahneman and his associates have shown that even so called "expert" intuitions by psychologists, stock traders, baseball scouts, and economists gives results that are no better than chance. We have an unwarranted arrogance about our powers of intuition. Previously we learned that we are biased in our fast thinking toward subconscious genetic impulses that may not serve us well today in modern society.

Humanism as a life stance promotes Type 2 or slow thinking. As children of the Enlightenment and of modernism, we value the use of reason and open-minded critical thinking. Some feminists have criticized this, saying we ignore the more intuitional and emotional aspects of our being. This is certainly true in some cases. My wife's instincts about how to raise children are far better than mine. Still, this doesn't have to be an either/or situation. As Robert Heller, a governor of the Federal Reserve System, said, "Never ignore a gut feeling, but never believe that it is enough." Using Type 2 thinking is hard work. It's a lot easier to just spout off your ungrounded prejudices with self-congratulatory confidence than to carefully consider the evidence and be willing to change your mind. It's a lot easier to give in to racism and tribalism in our dealing with other groups than to step back and widen our circle of compassion. Humanism is a hard calling, as many times we are trying to transcend our harmful, instinctual evolutionary drives.

One needs to be skeptical of intuition as a method of knowledge since it can be merely our prejudices speaking or a fancy way of saying, "My guess is." Much of what we now know to be true is counterintuitive. I wake to see the sun come up and "move" across the sky. Is it any wonder the ancients thought the earth was fixed and the sun was moving? Intuition is not always benevolent or true. Our racism and tribalism can be seen as instincts to enhance the survival of ourselves and those closest to us. Self-analysis has been shown, in many ways, to be one of the poorest methods of knowing ourselves.

Still, something is at work here. Most of us would make a "gut check" before making a major decision. Our propensity to rationalize needs a countering voice. The best of intuitions are those that effectively integrate our rational knowledge, our instinctual desires, our base of real experience, and our heartfelt emotions. Who would sensibly get married without a "gut check?" We call it wisdom when this subconscious, integrative insight seems to be in sync with a rational evaluation of the facts. We can never think our intuitions are enough by themselves, except in those unavoidable situations when a quick decision must be made on incomplete evidence.

One task of intuition is to quickly and subconsciously sift through rational alternatives without conscious distractions and then present choices by way of what feels right. Intuition is nature's survival tool. It enables us to make quick decisions based on simple, ingrained formulas. It is especially important when dealing directly with people. It gives us "emotional intelligence." Still, the truly self-aware person knows that intuitional knowledge is always provisional at best and is always subject to our worst prejudices.

Rationalism: Rationalism is an overall deductive theory that reason is in itself a source of knowledge superior to and independent of sense perceptions. The Enlightenment, as was mentioned in the previous chapter on history, substituted a faith in rationality over a faith in religion. That new, rational faith would empower individuals to know and to act on what was in their own best interests. There was confidence that rationality was a complete system of knowledge rather than just a tool of reason, and that it gave absolutely sure knowledge. I distinguish rationality from the broader term reason in this case, where rationality uses the intellect to build conclusions without any sense experience. It is the idea of knowing things through pure logic. Much of this confidence came from the deductive powers of mathematics. People generally find it a delight to see the awesome and sure powers of rationality, in geometry for example, by proving the Pythagorean Theorem. Mathematics truly is the language of the universe.

Without going into a long explanation involving centuries of critical examination, most philosophers now believe that rationalism is a very limited tool for knowledge. First of all, they found that rational statements such as "All dogs are canines" carry little new knowledge other than redescriptions of what we already know. These are called tautologies. Secondly, the only place that rationality seems to have any *pure* use appears to be in pure mathematics and in logic. Thirdly, any logical use of pure rationality involves setting up premises by which we come up with a logical syllogistic statement as:

> All dogs walk on all fours;
> My husband is a dog;
> Therefore, my husband walks on all fours.

This is, of course, absurd, but points out that if any of the premises are wrong, the conclusion will be wrong. Catholicism, for example, is one of the most rational of religions due to the Jesuits who have been working for centuries on their tortured logic. It all depends on your premises. But, what is to ground the premises?

Bertrand Russell and Alfred North Whitehead worked for over twenty years on their *Principia Mathematica* to prove that all of mathematics had firm foundations in logic. Kurt Gödel published a paper in 1931 that once and for all proved that a single Theory of Everything is actually impossible. Gödel proved conclusively, using mathematical logic itself, that "any such precise (formal) mathematical system of axioms and rules of procedure whatever, provided that it is broad enough to contain descriptions of simple arithmetic propositions . . . and is free from contradiction, must contain statements that are neither provable nor disprovable by the means allowed within the system." No formal system can be both consistent and complete, Gödel demonstrated. Any system of logic or numbers will *always* rest on at least a few unprovable assumptions.

For example, consider the classical "Liar's Paradox," which is the statement, "I am lying." This is self-contradictory, since if it's true, I'm not a liar, and it's false. If it's false, I am a liar, and so it's true.

What makes Gödel's Incompleteness Theorem even more revolutionary—why it is considered the twentieth century's greatest logical and mathematical achievement—is that it applies not just to math, but to everything that is subject to the laws of logic. Incompleteness is true in mathematics, but it's also true in language, science, and philosophy.

We now know that ultimately we have no absolute rational foundations for any of our premises. The philosopher John Dewey pointed out that there may well be absolute foundations, but we just don't know them absolutely. We are stuck in a world of anti-foundationalism with no logically complete "grand narratives." We have found that the curse of humankind actually has been the notion of absolute certainty. It is a curse we can and should overcome. We don't need certainty to gain knowledge.

It's true that logic and pure rationality may tell us some things about mathematics—something we will find useful as an evaluative tool within the scientific method. But logic and rationality, in and of themselves, tell us nothing about the really important things, such as who we are, what the world is like, and how to live our lives.

In historical practice, sadly, rationalism has led to narrow-minded ideology, orthodoxy and dogma. Catholicism, Communism, and Objectivism are all promoted as "rational systems." If you accept their premises, they are entirely rational. (I will have more to say about this later). Using purely rational thinking, people can feel they are absolutely right, are self-confident of their rationality, and then justify enormous errors in judgment. Rationality is not a complete system of knowledge, but merely one tool among many to discover the truth.

Science: The scientific method is not one method, but rather a group of techniques for discovering truth of the world. *Science is the systematic knowledge of the physical or material world gained through observation and experimentation, using logic to evaluate the results.* It is based on certain premises, such as: that the world is knowable, reasonable and uniform; the world can be represented by symbols; and our knowledge of the world is cumulative and progressive. We cannot be certain these premises are true, but the scientific method will assume they are true unless and until we find evidence to the contrary Still, we have not found any evidence that would contradict these premises, even when scanning the farthest galaxies.

Science takes various theories and subjects them to a battery of tests. It is a fierce battle of competing theories, pummeled by rational analysis, challenged by looking at all the facts, analyzed by alternative viewpoints, and forced to be both internally consistent and consistent with larger knowledge. Finally, a winner (or winners) emerges from this Darwinian struggle to find the fittest representation of reality. The struggle for survival of a theory over its rivals is never absolute, because science is always open to new viewpoints. Knowledge is always provisional; it is what survives when all the evidence has been critically examined and discredited theories are discarded. As William James said it, "Truth happens to an idea. It becomes true, is made true by events."

Science has three main functions, allowing us to:

1. Explain
2. Predict
3. Use the knowledge thereby gained in the world.

We see varying degrees for each function. For example, science has given us very detailed and complete explanations of the weather, but so far we have poor abilities to predict beyond around three days or to control it. Weather involves vast, complex systems of air, water, and land. We can explain the weather very well, but cannot predict it very well.

Conversely, quantum mechanics is the most proven scientific theory by which we can predict with incredible precision, but our explanations are virtually nil. Our inability to predict the behavior of subatomic particles, such as when a radioactive nucleus will decay, is inherent in quantum mechanics and not due to our limited information. Nevertheless, we can use quantum mechanics to calculate the magnetic field of an electron and the result agrees with measurements at an accuracy of ten decimal places. We may not be able to explain quantum mechanics, but it is extremely accurate. All electronic devices are based on quantum mechanics; every time you use a phone or computer you are confirming its correctness. Unlike the two extreme examples of the weather and quantum mechanics, most of our scientific knowledge has varying degrees of explanatory and predictive qualities.

Notably, science uses some of the other sources of what might be knowledge within its processes. Sometimes intuition can introduce a new theory. Einstein, for example, used intuition, by way of thought experiments, in much of his development of the theory of relativity. Also, a theory is expected to stand up to rational analysis by independent third parties. And lastly, the opinion of experts who have objectively studied the various theories may hold more weight than those who are not. But, in the final analysis, science is a communal, open-minded search for truth concerning the regularities of nature, using all the tools at our disposal that have been proven to work.

In the inductive method that most of us have learned, a scientist comes up with a hypothesis, develops an experiment to prove or falsify that hypothesis, makes the observations, and determines the probability that the hypothesis is true. Next, such findings are subjected to peer review and replication by other independent observers until there is a predominance of evidence in favor of the hypothesis—or until it is conclusively proven to be false. Generally, that is how it is supposed to work, but we know that this is only one of many such pathways to scientific knowledge.

Many attempts have been made to create a unifying theory of science but, so far, all have met with failure. The history of science has shown that, in actual practice, science seems to depend on many theories, but never has any single theory been found to apply in all situations. As the neurologist and self-proclaimed skeptic Dr. Steven Novella says, "Science is simply a systematic way for carefully observing nature and using consistent logic to evaluate results." (For a more complete discussion, see the fourth edition of A. F. Chalmers' *What Is This Thing Called Science*.)

Think of it this way. When you go into a garage to fix something, you will not find one tool that does everything. Similarly, we have many scientific tools at our disposal and for most projects we will use several of them. We always want to try to look at the evidence, but sometimes, as in Einstein's thought experiments, there is no immediate evidence. We try to design an experiment to falsify an idea, but sometimes there is no way to do this. Theories rise in proportion to their successes, not because of the failures of other theories.

What are some of those tools or tests we use in science? Here are some critical thinking tools:

- Ask for sufficient evidence.
- Ask for a theory to be testable and falsifiable.
- Extraordinary claims require extraordinary evidence.
- We should accept an extraordinary hypothesis only if no ordinary one will do.
- All things being equal, the simplest hypothesis is the best one (Occam's Razor).
- All things being equal, the best hypothesis is the one that is most conservative and agrees with already established beliefs.
- Be skeptical of beliefs that disagree with expert opinion, established theories, established facts, or logic; or that rely on "faith," personal attacks, obfuscating language, damning the origin, appeals to authority, or double-talk.
- Theories cannot be argued in isolation, because prior assumptions matter.

These are not all of them, but this list does give you an idea of the common-sense tools that have been found to work. In Appendix 3 we will go into more detail. Civilization has collected a number of these time-tested critical thinking tools. We need them because we know we can be biased, and it is hard to always be objective or not to plead our own special case. These tools can help overcome some of our inherent deficiencies at getting to the truth. None of the tools of critical intelligence is totally sufficient and none is totally conclusive.

Science is not always pleasant. As the seventeenth-century French writer François Duc de La Rochefoucauld said, "There is nothing more horrible than the murder of a beautiful theory by a brutal gang of facts." In the end, truth is what's left when we get rid of all the lies.

Science, while always urging us to be open-minded, is not always a positive process. Generally, science is a process of falsification. As the ancient Greek playwright Euripides said, "Man's most valuable trait is a judicious sense of what not to believe." Doubt is a powerful tool, as long as it doesn't descend into cynicism, nihilism, or relativism. As Thomas Jefferson said, "Reason and free inquiry are the only effectual agents against error."

An immense satisfaction results when, as a scientist, one fully analyzes all the evidence and alternative theories and can point to one as a winner.

With the scientific method, the door is never closed to new ideas. Also, there is no talk of absolute certainty. Knowledge doesn't require certainty. It is always contingent on the best facts available and the best-available interpretation of those facts. The scientific mind endeavors to resist fixed notions of what is true. Instead, it is wedded to a process of critical, disciplined intelligence. It operates as a collective enterprise that cumulatively and progressively builds a knowledge base. That base of knowledge frequently must be rebuilt in spots.

I remember my first time in a graduate science seminar seeing a lot of very bright people tackle a difficult subject, trying to find some flaw, some opening for other theories. I saw people change their positions in a heartbeat, without embarrassment, when proven wrong. They were delighted when a new idea seemed to have merit. This taught me something about the nobility of scientific character.

The philosopher Willard Quine talks of a "web of belief" that each of us holds, which is why scientific ideas should have coherence with other proven ideas. His point is that all our ideas are interrelated, interconnected, and mutually supporting. Additionally, the eighteenth-century English philosopher Thomas Bayes pointed out that all our ideas are built on prior probability assumptions. Rocket scientists assume, with good confidence, that Newton's theory of gravity is correct when they complete their calculations, but it is all the probabilities added together that give us an overall probability that what they are doing is correct.

One can take a commitment to science too narrowly. A group of people called the Logical Positivists said only statements that can be empirically verified should be considered as true. But then the question arose: what empirically verifies that fundamental statement itself? It doesn't logically follow. As we have seen, developing reliable scientific knowledge is more complex than we originally thought.

Another consideration stemming from a scientific worldview is the free will vs. determination controversy. Determinists typically view the world as a bottom-up, cause-and-effect process, which makes them ask, how can humans have free will? Is everything we think and do merely a result of our biological and cultural history? Are we just kidding ourselves by thinking we are freely making decisions? This deep, complex question has not yet been satisfactorily answered and it may never be in our lifetimes, although we continue now and then to pick off little pieces.

Many of the philosophers in this area hold to a view that free will can be compatible with cause and effect, a view called "compatibilism." We don't have time or space to delve into this intellectual quagmire, but I suggest side-stepping it for now and thinking of it this way. Free will isn't something we "have," it's something we practice. We don't know exactly how much of what we believe in comes from human agency and how much is just a result of complex hidden process and history. We do know we need to at least act like volition is a useful pragmatic construct in our lives. There is strong scientific evidence for doing so.

When test subjects were indoctrinated not to believe in free will, they lied, cheated, and stole more. This was in a study by Kathleen Vohs, then at the University of Utah, and Jonathan Schooler, of the University of Pittsburgh. Rejecting free will increases aggression and mindless conformity. It leads to less critical thinking and ultimately to an acquiescent fatalism. In the absence of strong arguments one way or another, philosophers have promoted a belief in free will because it works. The last thing we need, in a world plagued by problems, is to give up.

So what ultimately grounds science, especially if it is true that there are no absolute foundations to anything we may believe? (This idea is called anti-foundationalism.) The philosopher Otto Neurath gave us a metaphor to think of scientific knowledge as a boat that we must rebuild while at sea. We replace boards and plug leaks—errors—but can't get off to fix these leaks on a firm, dry platform. We have cranes to help us plug leaks and rebuild; these tools are science, experience and reason. All these allow us to make a stronger boat that gets better with time. There are no certain, ultimate foundations and nothing is the certain premise of all the arguments. Still, all the arguments must fit together in Quine's "web of belief." This is called "coherentism." The boat won't "float" unless all the ideas work as a whole.

Putting everything together we find all knowledge has three main features; specifically, it is *fallible, tentative, and probabilistic.* Ultimately, why should one believe that science has valid methods for finding the truth? For two very important reasons: it works, and it is the only self-regulating method of knowledge. Regardless what its detractors say about it, science delivers the goods.

Civilization: Civilization is an advanced state of human society, in which a high level of culture, science, industry, and government has been reached. Civilization is a repository of the ideas and practices that historically have served us best. Civilization includes other good stuff that is necessary along with science.

Science, for all its power and utility, has dangers. One can become so enamored with it that a narrow ideology called "scientism" develops. Scientism is the overdependence on science to guide our lives. One can become so reductive as to miss seeing the emergence of overarching complex systems. It is ridiculous to see love as merely a neurochemical mental process, computer programs as nothing but compilers of ones and zeros, or democracy as a system of counting votes.

Complex systems build whole new levels of reality. We need not focus on only the infinitesimally small or the complex macro systems. It seems to me we that we have a responsibility to understand all aspects and all levels of reality. I can and do appreciate the elegance of the DNA coding in a plant as well as how a flower's form ensures that bees carry its pollen to another plant. Additionally, I can appreciate how a flower can transfix my gaze and speak of an elegance no words can describe; how its scent can remind us of long-ago memories of summer. Only the narrow-minded do not consider a holistic view of the world. As the American artist Louis Orr said, "Science will never be able to reduce the value of a sunset to arithmetic. Nor can it reduce friendship to formula. Laughter and love, pain and loneliness, the challenge of beauty and truth: these will always surpass the scientific mastery of nature."

Later we will discuss the role of civilization in more depth, along with its role in guiding our knowledge base and our lives.

No way – postmodernism: In recent years a large school of thought identified as postmodernism has gained influence, at least in academic circles. Most do not know how it has permeated all our culture. It has become the water we swim in. It originated in European Marxist thought, in which reason and science were seen as tools for capitalists to dominate and control. Postmodernists argued that reason was inherently hierarchical, promoting—all by itself—oppressive bureaucracies and even fascism. Others saw our so-called "scientific objectivity" as a cover-up for a highly prejudicial process in the service of white male power interests against minorities.

Several examples show that the postmodernists had no trouble making their case. Until 1973, for instance, the American Psychiatric Association classified homosexuality as a mental disorder. The psychologist Bruno Bettelheim thought autism in children was caused by insufficient love from their mothers. In the last century, black people were held to have lower mental ability because of their brain size. In each of these cases, bogus "science" backed up the proponents' prejudicial views that were later proven untrue. Historically, bad science has led to and given credence to some horrible injustices. On a positive note, it was scientists who uncovered these horrific errors and corrected them.

An example given by postmodernists of rationality as an oppressive tool is the Pruitt-Igoe low-income housing project in St. Louis, near where I grew up. The project's outward rationality was to provide clean, affordable housing for the poor. This project and others like it failed disastrously, as they concentrated massive social problems and became gang war zones. What these high-rise slums actually were was a way to warehouse low-income blacks out of sight and out of mind, reduce white guilt, and treat the poor as prisoners in concentrated zoos under the guise of rational city planning. The projects' technocratic rationality did not consider the complex human issues and masked the hidden racism. The Pruitt-Igoe projects began to be demolished in 1972, which some consider the beginning of the Postmodern era.

In the area of linguistics, postmodernists saw language as entirely relative and masking hidden agendas. One could "deconstruct" literature to find underlying meanings about the authors' subconscious motives for power and control.

In physics, such difficult theoretical concepts as relativity, quantum mechanics, Werner Heisenberg's uncertainty principle, and chaos theory have been used to justify the notion that all of science—and reality itself—is relative, strange, and inherently unknowable. In philosophy, it is argued that there are no foundations for any truth and that one idea is as good as the next. Some second-wave feminists claim that reasoning is only a male tool for their power and control, and that women's intuition better serves them and society as a whole. Ultimately, the postmodernists argue, there are no foundations for anything we believe and all knowledge is a social construction.

At the outset, let me state that many of these arguments have some element of truth about them, but many are unsubstantiated. Much of postmodernist thought is based on taking good ideas to their illogical extremes. Each argument must be judged on its own merit, so let's do exactly that with a few of the most important ones.

First, let's deal with our subjectivity. We all have a marvelous ability to lie to ourselves about our subconscious motivations. There is no doubt that much of our thinking is subconsciously biased. As William James said, "Most of us think we are thinking when we are merely rearranging our prejudices." We are woefully ignorant of how we bend reason to our own smug self-interest. We can be more rationalizing animals than rational ones. We can all fall prey to the "confirmation bias" whereby we cherry-pick data that confirms our prejudices.

Can we rise above these subconscious manipulations? The scientific method strives for objectivity by using self-correcting communal checks and balances. Some techniques that help achieve scientific objectivity are double-blind studies, independent review, confirmation of findings, and controlling experiments to isolate them from outside influences. These methods do not always eliminate prejudice, but one thing is certain—someone will always be willing to find any errors or biases we may have and make a name for themselves by debunking a proposition. Yes, humans have a highly subjective nature, which we never can fully overcome. But critical analysis by others provides the correctives required for building reliable knowledge.

Does science itself say the world is entirely relative, as some have proposed? Some have said quantum mechanics shows the total "craziness" of our universe and the fact that an "observer" determines the outcome of any process. Without entering a long digression on what is called "indeterminacy," I would just point out that the quantum mechanical "weirdness" occurs only at the subatomic level and not the "macro" level where we live our daily lives.

Heisenberg's uncertainty principle is used to explain why the universe is—well—uncertain. What is ironic about using this example to justify the "relativity of knowledge" is that it is, in fact, one of the most thoroughly and precisely known physical principles. The "uncertainty" in Heisenberg's principle is an exact and well-tested statement about the limits and tradeoffs of measurement. Some calculations based on quantum mechanics agree with experimental results to ten decimal places! A good example of what "uncertainty" in physics means: if an electron (or any other object) has a very well defined momentum, its position is necessarily uncertain.

Many think this is a nail in the coffin of determinism, an idea that led to the claim that the future would be absolutely predictable if we knew the present positions and motions of all atoms, but some do not. Heisenberg's principle, one of the foundations of quantum mechanics, says absolute determinism of the future is impossible. Another example of indeterminacy is that it is impossible to predict when a particular radioactive atom will decay. One can only state the probability that it will decay in any given time interval. This also tells us why atoms don't collapse into themselves.

All modern electronic devices are based on the correctness of quantum mechanics. Far from showing how little we know, it is an excellent example of the orderliness of nature and our ability to determine its structure and how it operates.

Newton's law of gravitation is not exact. It's good enough, usually, but it goes wrong when speeds get close to the speed of light or when gravitational fields get very big. Einstein's general relativity supersedes it in these cases. Newton's law is not "wrong," but it has its limits. While the general theory of relativity was a product of Einstein's deep thinking, it still had to be confirmed by observation. Proofs that Einstein was correct included observations of the planet Mercury's perihelion shift, and the bending of distant starlight by the sun's gravity.

The general theory of relativity only recently had its first practical application. Every time one uses a GPS device or flies in an airplane, you are relying on general relativity for corrections to your position. That is because in fast-orbiting satellites clocks tick faster than those on Earth. This is a great example of a theory having all three characteristics of science: explanation, prediction, and real use in practice.

We could examine more of the postmodern beliefs, but ultimately they have been shown to be the result of taking good (and useful) ideas to their irrational extreme. It is true that much of our knowledge becomes biased by needs of power and control. But it does not follow that we

have no knowledge. It is true that various writings have
many possible interpretations. It does not follow that an
author has no valid point to make. It is true that science
has made some grievous errors. It does not follow that
science is not progressively learning from those errors. It
is true that language can influence our thinking. It does
not follow that all knowledge is relative to our language.
It is true that reason has been used, and continues to be
used, as a tool for oppression. It does not follow that we
should abandon it, or, as the linguist Noam Chomsky
said, "Then only the rich and powerful will have it."

Postmodernism has been largely discredited and is on
the wane. Even some of its most ardent followers are dis-
avowing it. As the English historian Richard Evans said,
"Of course it is right to say that we can never know the
whole or absolute truth about anything in the past. But,
just because we can never attain the whole or absolute
truth, just because we make mistakes in our search for
the truth about the past, just because there will always
be something new to say about any historical subject, it
does not follow that there is no such thing as the truth
at all." To its credit, however, postmodernism teaches us
always to beware of our prejudices and thus is a counter
to our hubris.

Postmodernism has been termed *Fashionable Nonsense*,
from the book of the same name by Alan Sokal and Jean
Bricmont, which exposed its hollowness. Postmodernism
is quickly decaying in important academic circles, but
its pernicious effects linger throughout academia and
the general culture. Even one of its greatest exponents,
Terry Eagleton, who wrote the postmodern classic *Literary
Theory*, recently wrote a refutation titled *After Theory*. He

saw that he was going to be on the wrong side of history and rushed to the exit.

Postmodern thinking is an extreme form of subjectivism and cynicism that subtly took over much of general culture. There is much to inform us within postmodern thought, but ultimately it is like a petulant child who wants knowledge pure and certain, and if it can't be obtained, pouts, throws a temper tantrum and walks away.

Don't listen to what people say; watch what they do. If you want to see hypocrisy, watch a postmodernist board a scientifically designed airplane. You only believe in something strongly if you would bet your life on it. As some have pointed out, there are no postmodernists at forty thousand feet.

Pragmatism: Humanism has historically been closely allied with pragmatism as another way of looking at knowledge. Pragmatism considered that with all the problems of gaining knowledge, it might be best to look at what knowledge is actually successful. The pragmatic outlook considers the outcomes, that is, what has "cash value" or real worth in the end. The great American philosopher John Dewey, one of the signers of the Humanist Manifesto, asked that a claim of knowledge have "warranted assertability." In this regard, pragmatism asks us not so much to focus on a specific methodology, but to look at what works in real life. While pluralistic in its methodology, pragmatism most closely allies itself with science and its self-correcting methods. Some have pointed out that pragmatists get it backwards. Ideas may work because they are true, not true because they work. Yet there is something to be gained in keeping an eye on what works. John Dewey presciently envisioned science developing a better understanding of what works for our benefit, both as individuals and as a society.

Epistemic pluralism: Some natural phenomena cannot be fully explained by a single theory or fully investigated using a single approach. My own inclination for gaining truth is towards epistemic or synoptic pluralism. That is a pragmatic, scientific realism that uses a pluralism of methods. The philosopher Ludwig Wittgenstein, harkening back to Socrates, used the metaphor of a braided rope, which we use to climb toward greater knowledge. The strands in the rope are incomplete and none can carry the load by itself, but together they build a stronger, more resilient, and longer rope that reaches higher and higher. "It does not get its strength from any fiber which runs through it from one end to the other, but from the fact that there is a vast number of fibers overlapping."

Let's use all the best and reliable tools for gaining knowledge, keeping humble as we always may be biased and wrong, but confident that history shows we are slowly and progressively advancing our knowledge using reason. Truth is unfolding. Classical modernism overreached in its ideas about progress, especially in human affairs. Nevertheless, in the twenty-first century we are indeed fulfilling many of our dreams of understanding the world. Reason and science are still our best ways to discover knowledge of the world. We will discuss these results in the next chapter.

Having reviewed the various approaches, we can say the following things about how best to find knowledge.

Summary of Some Modern Knowledge Beliefs

1. There are no absolute first principles or foundations for any belief system (anti-foundationalism).
2. Yes, there may be absolutes, especially with the laws of logic. We just can't know them absolutely. Absolute certainty on anything is closure of the free mind.
3. Truth building is generally, but not always, a negative process by which various ideas are tested using critical intelligence. Rival theories compete against each other in a Darwinian battle.
4. All truth-making is tainted by our subconscious needs, especially for power and control. We must always humble ourselves due to our own and others' subjectivity and biases.
5. Science is the only self-correcting method that allows us to explain, predict, and control our world. There is no one scientific method; it is more like a tool box.
6. Reason and science are our best, but not only, methods of obtaining truth. Truth-building is linked with all aspects of living.
7. Truth is what is left when we get rid of all the lies.
8. Pragmatism combined with scientific realism, using many knowledge tools, appears to be the best overall methodology. Pragmatism is the rope of knowledge in applied action. An epistemic pluralism of methods provides many tools by which we can succeed in gaining truth.
9. The primary tests for truth ask if an idea is coherent, is non-contradictory, and is consistent with the facts (reality). These tests may not always work.

10. We have a predisposition to belief. Skepticism in all things is required; yet we must land on some beliefs even if tentatively.

11. Knowledge is best viewed as tentative, fallible, probabilistic, the best approximation of reality, and always open to revision.

12. Appeals to revelation and ungrounded authority are unacceptable, because they are arbitrary.

13. All knowledge is open to review; no area is taboo.

14. There are many areas in life where there is no "right" answer—and that's OK.

15. Science has grounding by "bootstrapping" itself. It grounds itself because it works.

16. Pure logic has some limited grounding because of self-consistent tautologies. Pure rationalism is a highly questionable method due to the problem of ungrounded and prejudiced premises.

17. The source of ideas is different than proving them and producing knowledge; for example, art, intuition, religious experience, etc. can provide ideas, insights and motivation, but do not constitute proven knowledge except as experiential knowledge.

18. Experiential knowledge is still important, because our consciousness is ourselves looking at and experiencing the world.

19. Unusual claims require unusually tough evidence.

20. Each of us holds a "web of belief" (Willard Quine). All our ideas are interconnected and interdependent.

21. Think of scientific knowledge as a boat that we must rebuild while at sea. We replace boards and plug leaks (errors), but can't get off to fix them on a firm,

dry foundation. We have cranes to help us rebuild (science, experience and reason) and make a stronger boat that gets better with time (Otto Neurath).

22. It is helpful to separate facts from values while realizing that they really inform each other.

23. Civilization is the repository of all the knowledge that works best for us.

24. These are the views of one person, trying to summarize where the study of knowledge is today, but they are bound to be revised in time. Some may disagree with parts of it. Study this field yourself.

In the next chapter let's try to put together what we know about the facts of the world that seem to be true. Later we will deal with the subject of values.

6

What We Know

In the last chapter we discussed how we gain knowledge. Now let's discuss what we know about the facts of the world. Religion provides a whole set of answers about where we came from, where we are going, and what it means to be human, but we Humanists through all the tools (especially science) mentioned in the last chapter have also formulated answers to these questions.

This universe began some 13.7 billion years ago from a singularity leading to a big bang, a huge inflationary explosion. We know this back to about 10-42 seconds after the universe's creation, before which the fabric of space-time reduces to "quantum foam," the standard laws of physics start to break down and there is no temporal order. Over millions and millions of years, the universe has continued to expand and arrange into everything that we experience today.

But in recent years, a revolution in physics is changing our views about how the universe came into being.

As the physicist Lawrence Krauss wrote, "Discoveries of modern particle physics and cosmology over the past half century allow not only a possibility that the universe arose from nothing, but in fact make this possibility increasingly plausible. Everything we have measured about the universe is not only consistent with a universe that came from nothing (and didn't have to turn out this way!) but, in fact, all the new evidence makes this possibility ever more likely."

The old idea that nothing can evolve from empty space, devoid of mass, energy, or anything material, has now been replaced by a boiling bubbling brew of virtual particles, popping in and out of existence in a time so short that we cannot detect them directly. "Nothing"—beyond merely empty space—including the absence of space itself, and even the absence of physical laws, can morph into "something." Indeed, in modern parlance, "nothing" is most often unstable. Not only can something arise from nothing, but often the laws of physics require this to occur given that energy always contains a certain amount of uncertainty, even in a vacuum.

This is a far more fascinating story of our genesis than, well, Genesis. We may never know the origin of the universe. It is way too soon to claim that this is the fully accepted scientific theory of the universe's beginnings, but it is interesting to speculate.

The great underlying story about the universe is that it is self-created and self-organizing. This is one of the most important insights of modern science, that it is a bottom-up, not top down, story. It is an emergent universe, with all the wonderful complexity emerging out of simpler forms. As the universe expanded and cooled, subatomic particles coalesced into larger ones, then into hydrogen, and then into stars, where in their high temperatures the heavier elements were formed. It takes a tremendous amount of energy to get beyond the element iron, so we know that one or more of these stars collapsed into itself, creating a supernova. In the process, all the elements with atomic weights greater than iron's were created. If you have a gold ring, it is the ashes of a star that exploded billions of years ago. The earth itself is 4.54 billion years old.

In graduate school we theoretically calculated what the relative occurrence of elements on Earth would be, just using the known temperature of stars when they went supernova, along with the strong and weak nuclear forces. In elegant precision, the theoretical distribution of elements exactly matches what we actually find on Earth. It is such a beautiful example of how science gives us such bold, confident tools for understanding our world. In this case, we actually develop one proof that we are stardust looking back at the universe.

A graduate student can get cocky with this sort of powerful predictive and explanatory power. Conversely, it is in studying the subatomic world that a scientist is humbled. Einstein's curved space-time theory of relativity tells us that motion in space has no absolute meaning. Heisenberg's uncertainty principle tells us a subatomic particle cannot have both location and momentum until one or the other is measured, and this uncertainty isn't just a matter of our measuring tools.

The weirdness of quantum mechanics seems to show that measuring subatomic events has a "spooky action at a distance" that is dependent on an observation, and the observation doesn't even have to be human. Albert Einstein himself rejected this quantum weirdness and the particle/ wave duality. Along with colleagues Boris Podolsky and Nathan Rosen, he posed the so-called EPR experiment— from the initials of the investigators' last names—that he hoped would settle the matter. Einstein was decisively proven wrong three decades later when John Bell showed that some phenomena, such as spin of a particle, cannot have certain properties until they are measured. Again, this isn't just a result of the measurement device. It is due to the indeterminacy inherent in reality until an observation measures something and "collapses the wave function," to use the language of some quantum mechanics specialists.

The reality of our universe gets more mystifying and strange the more we look at it. Matter isn't really "solid," but it is itself a wave function. We are used to basing our lives on cause-and-effect relationships, when in fact quantum mechanics shows that things occur all the time at the subatomic level that are indeterminate and possibly spontaneous. Watches with glow-in-the-dark hands glow because radium 226 spontaneously decays into radon 222 and an alpha particle. Nothing can be said to "cause" any of those radium atoms to decay.

We may inhabit the only universe or we may be one of a number (greater than 10^{80}) of universes. Our universe may have spontaneously erupted on "quantum foam." It gets weirder if one considers the very real possibility that our universe may be just a computer simulation, maybe one among billions of others. This is not as far-fetched as it sounds when one considers that we would have no way of actually knowing the truth.

Whew. Even physicists get dizzy contemplating our universe's crazy weirdness. You don't have to understand all of this to know a few things. The reality of the universe is far stranger than can be imagined. Some New Agers like Deepak Chopra and even Christian apologists I have debated are using quantum weirdness to justify ideas of God and relativism. They say that because modern science has shown everything is relative, you should just believe in God. But it just doesn't logically follow that God must exist, simply because the subatomic universe is weird.

I'll reiterate this important basic fact: quantum weirdness does not occur at the macro level we live in, but is generally just at the subatomic level or—in the new language—when "quantum entanglement from complexity" occurs. One recent experiment showed macro-level entanglement took place when no other interactions occur between two objects at a distance from each other. Still, this really doesn't matter for our purposes at the macro level. Matter may not be really "solid" in quantum mechanical terms, but the door I ran into today felt pretty solid to me.

Quantum weirdness also doesn't negate scientific knowledge at the macro level. We can still confidently calculate the momentum and the location of a baseball—Newton's four-hundred-year-old laws of motion work just fine for that purpose—even if we just can't do the same for an electron. I fully expect future revolutions in Quantum Mechanics .that will up end changing much of what I have written here. I find that exciting, not threatening.

Moving on to biology, the first self-replicating molecules emerged and then life began around four billion years ago. Highly evolved multicellular life forms, similar to those we know today, appeared during the Paleozoic period around 542 to 488 million years ago. Around six million years ago, primates split into the evolutionary lines that led to chimpanzees and our human ancestors. The brain size of the humanoid line expanded greatly; fire was first used sometime between 1.5 million and eight hundred thousand years ago. The earliest modern humans (*Homo sapiens*) were living in Africa around two hundred to four hundred thousand years ago, but it is amazing that at least four humanoid species coexisted as late as forty thousand years ago. Our human species almost became extinct between ninety thousand and sixty thousand years ago. The number of reproductively active adults was reduced to between one hundred and ten thousand individuals, possibly due to environmental stresses caused by climate change or a volcanic explosion. This explains why all human beings are so genetically similar, more so than most other species. Through the process of evolution, we humans developed self-aware big brains that can create cities, cell phones, hope, love, and religion.

As the Humanist minister and poet Robert Weston described it:

> *Out of the stars in their flight, out of the dust of eternity, here have we come,*
>
> *Stardust and sunlight, mingling through time and through space.*
>
> *Out of the stars have we come, up from time.*
> *Out of the stars have we come.*
>
> *Time out of time before time in the vastness of space, earth spun to orbit the sun,*

Earth with the thunder of mountains newborn, the boiling
of seas.

Earth warmed by sun, lit by sunlight;
This is our home;
Out of the stars have we come.

Mystery hidden in mystery, back through all time;
Mystery rising from rocks in the storm and the sea.

Out of the stars, rising from rocks and the sea, kindled by
sunlight on earth, arose life.

Ponder this thing in your heart, life up from sea:
Eyes to behold, throats to sing, mates to love.

Life from the sea, warmed by sun, washed by rain, life from
within, giving birth,
rose to love.

This is the wonder of time;
this is the marvel of space;
out of the stars swung the earth;
life upon earth rose to love.

This is the marvel of life, rising to see and to know;
Out of your heart, cry wonder:
sing that we live.

Evolution is an amazing process. It's how successful
characteristics are spread through members of a population
by parents who were better able to survive and reproduce.
It's astounding to think that every one of your ancestors
survived and reproduced and that at least some of their
children went on to survive and reproduce as well. Only
those whose ancestors successfully adapted to their envi-

ronments are here today. Here are Darwin's final words from his book, On the *Origin of Species*:

"There is grandeur in this view of life, with its several powers, having been originally breathed by the Creator into a few forms or into one; and that, whilst this planet has gone cycling on according to the fixed law of gravity, from so simple a beginning endless forms most beautiful and most wonderful have been and are being evolved."

There is little difference in kind or degree between the chimpanzees and ourselves. Language, abstract thinking, and reflective awareness are areas where humans seem to have significant and important differences from our nearest animal relatives. One thing is fairly certain. Only humans have the ability to consciously and significantly change the world. This lends a special responsibility to our species.

Our biological evolution took place and our genetic heritage was forged over millions of years on the African savannas. Our cultural evolution occurred around the globe and created modern civilization. That is a very recent phenomenon compared to the Darwinian impulses that built up while our ancestors were hunter-gatherers living in small tribes. We are a naked, tribal ape with all the old Stone Age impulses for reproduction and survival now trying to adapt culturally to modern life and all its complexity. The interaction between our twin aspects of nature and nurture makes the two impossible to tease apart.

For much of the twentieth century it was thought that there was no firm human nature and that we were infinitely

malleable. That was ideological nonsense. Humanist of
the Year in 2009 Steven Pinker gives a full account in his
book *The Blank Slate*. While biology is not destiny, it creates powerful drives, proclivities, and impulses toward
certain behaviors linked to survival and reproduction.
These impulses are largely subconscious.

The philosopher and 2004 Humanist of the Year Daniel
Dennett concluded that Darwin's great idea is a universal
acid (a metaphor) that can dissolve almost all philosophical problems. This is a little bit overstated, but Darwinism
helps us see how our genetic drives influence not just our
nature, but the nurture aspects of humans as well. The
American anthropologist Donald Brown has found over
two hundred traits that he calls human universals, which
are found in every culture. There is, evidence shows, a
fundamental human nature.

The Stone Age impulses imbedded within us can be
problematic. Tribalism, sexism, racism, violence, religion,
desires for sweet and fatty foods, and high birthrates served
us well on the African plains, but are poorly adaptive traits
for modern life. Fortunately for our survival, another great
evolutionary emergence is now countering our biological
nature. That is the emergence of civilization.

Civilization, as the emergent cultural memory of a
people, is a repository of good ideas, technologies and
practices that actually work. Our ideas of democracy that
have developed over time have proven worth. The nuances
of representative democracy emerged out of those ideas.
Instincts toward tribalism and war have been controlled
where possible by the concept of equal moral worth and
tolerance. Our knowledge of medical issues has tempered
our instincts to load up on fat. Civilization is a combina-

tion of all the technical, scientific and cultural capital we have gained over time; it is a tapestry that holds our societies together.

Narrowly looking only at the natural aspects of our being can allow us to rationalize such harmful traits as Social Darwinism, sexism, and tribalism. On the other hand, thinking our biological nature can be completely overwhelmed by culture has resulted in utopian thinking such as Communism. The failure in Russia, over a bloody three-quarters of a century, to mold a "new Soviet man" is a stark reminder that human nature isn't easily changed. The same could be said about strained efforts to argue there is no real difference between men and women. We are products of both nature and nurture and all the entanglements of each. The real question for us is to determine what emotional drives out of our old limbic brain, originally formed for survival and reproduction in Africa, remain useful and should be enhanced. The other side of that question is which traits should be rejected and controlled by cultural wisdom, which comes out of our neocortex. Our inner apes and our noble selves are in constant tension. They need constant controlling and balance if we are to grasp the ring and become the best we can be, both as individuals and a society.

Throughout the rest of this book I will return to the belief that this is a bottom-up, self-organizing and emergent universe. Self-organizing processes are all around us. Humanity, born of this emergent universe, emergent evolution and emergent culture, becomes the maker of meaning and values. We are under constant tension between our duality of nature and nurture, between our biological drives and civilization's noblest achievements.

We are an amazing biological artifact that somehow became a conscious entity; we are made of stardust that can look up and observe stardust and even contemplate the process whereby stardust became us. Our recursive, reflective, self-conscious brains are our personality. Our consciousness emerges from our brain and when we die, our personality dies with us. Some have illusions of immortality and of unembodied souls, but all the evidence points to body/brain death eliminating who we are.

From all we know, this world is all there is. There are no gods, ghosts, hereafter, or other magic. We have looked for evidence of the supernatural and have found none. Moreover, the laws of the universe as they apply here on earth appear to be consistent across the whole universe. This is why Humanists embrace naturalism, not because we can "prove" naturalism, but because it is the best we know. What we have here is it.

Some are concerned about subatomic weirdness, but in our daily lives, we human beings don't live in a subatomic "weird" world. We still find the truth in lives that are mortal, love that sustains us, bodies that leak, wounds that hurt, the earth's beauty and all the other things we find meaningful in the here and now. Sure, underlying all of life is a deep mystery about what is real, how the universe started, and how to live our lives. But unlike living a life focused on a supernatural hereafter or subatomic weirdness, we Humanists live confident lives centered on the best that we know that is true in the real world.

7

What Matters

Values are guideposts, marking what is important to us to help decide our future actions. They are stakes in the ground by which we mark off what we think is fundamentally important and what matters. There are many criticisms of any examination of values. Some say values are totally relative, or lacking a foundation, or deterministic, or that emotional preferences are merely the product of our biology and our culture. Further, they say there is nothing objective about our values. Is that so? Do we have to descend into relativistic nihilism and despair if we look too deeply? What merits our regard? We have already found that, for everything known about the world, there are no absolute foundations. Disturbingly, at first glance it appears the same is true about values.

From all we know, we live in a meaningless, self-created universe that one day will exhaust itself of energy and life. Does this realization make a mockery of our lives, of meaning and purpose, of all values? Does it demand, as our detractors say, that ultimately we have no other choice but nihilism, a valueless existence that negates all we hold dear?

These are serious accusations that deserve serious consideration. Do impermanence and mortality render all values ultimately worthless? For most of us, the reality is that we will be forgotten after two generations. Our graves will not be visited. No one will weep for us. A few of us may have left a legacy of something important, but very few of us. For most of us, death brings the quick forgetting that we ever lived.

Some think that mortality denies any meaning to life, but I think it increases it. The actor and comedian Ricky Gervais said, "It's a strange myth that atheists have nothing to live for. It's the opposite. We have nothing to die for. We have everything to live for." Once we give up the notion that meaning is tied to eternity, once we realize that this world is all there is, and once we realize that meaning is given and chosen in the moment of now, we begin to recognize meaning that emerges right here, right now.

Meaning and values aren't "out there" in the world. They come from within us. Choosing our values is our way to describe what matters for the future and how we will gauge our behavior. While meaning is bound to the present, values are forward-looking.

Over the centuries, many people have dealt with the issue of how we can find meaning without certainty, eternity, or immortality. One of the hallmark tenets of Buddhism is that suffering stems from a desire for permanence. By accepting impermanence and letting go of things, we can find meaning in the now. The western Stoics found the same wisdom.

There is a story, which may or may not be true, but its literal truth doesn't matter. The story embodies the concept of flux, change, and impermanence and how we can deal with them.

The story goes that a group of Buddhist monks spent some weeks at a suburban shopping mall making a mandala, a huge sand painting on the floor, with exquisite skill, form and fine detail. It is normal for them to destroy the painting when they are finished, to signify the Buddhist philosophy that nothing is permanent, neither in the world nor in our own lives.

When the mandala was nearly complete, some teenage boys came running through the mall, purposely scuffing their feet through the mandala, then running away. The Western onlookers were horrified and angry, but then the Buddhist monks immediately proceeded to scuff their feet through the painting as well, laughing and joking. The contrast of reactions couldn't have been starker between the Western mind, built on the concept of permanence, and the Eastern mind, accepting the reality of the impermanence of all things. The varied reactions stemmed from differing ideas about the source of meaning and happiness. The stoic Epictetus observed that our thoughts control our emotions. He wrote around 100 CE, "Men are disturbed not by things, but by the view which they take of them."

When we are mindfully aware, we indeed can find meaning in the here and now, the eternal present. This meaning dissolves any nihilism we might hold. Meaning is captured in the present by us human beings, the meaning makers.

Let us next examine the sources of our values and which of them, if any, may have intrinsic, universal, objective, or even higher value. We know that values can be highly subjective. Cultural values shape much of our value structure as do our biological impulses, but we typically also have an intertwined mix of both. We are complex, irreducible mixtures of bio-psycho-social proclivities, all interacting and intertwined and difficult to tease apart. We are torn by our own agency and psychology, our biological drives, and our cultural heritage.

As we learned earlier, we are biologically imprinted with value structures that help us survive and reproduce. Evolutionary psychology teaches us that we are social animals who value close relationships, children, compassion, sex, justice, love, stability, courage, storytelling, and food. On the other hand, the biologist E. O. Wilson pointed out, we are also instinctually wired for what he calls our "Paleolithic Curse." By that he means our evolutionary proclivities toward racism, sexism, violence, power and control, and fear of the other "tribe," all of which served us well on the plains of Africa a hundred thousand years ago, but are poorly suited for life in modern society's concrete jungles.

Racism is a good example of how biological fear of the "other tribe" and a culturally learned process mutually amplify each other. Still, twenty-five hundred years of civilization have taught us that racism harms everyone and that honoring each person's worth and dignity works better toward happiness for all. We can choose to reject prejudice and to value and accept everyone regardless of race.

Our biological proclivities are overlaid with other highly varied cultural values. Modern culture is increasingly shaped by economic and media culture. We are bombarded by paid advertising that tells us what values should be important to us. With capitalism, those supposed values are tied to products and services that can be bought or sold. We are told we can't be happy unless we have the latest smart phone, running shoe, or financial service. How many television advertisements have you seen that directly extol the value of love, critical reasoning, play, the beauty of a flower, and intimate relationships, unless they are exploiting them and referring to a product or service? Not many, because these values can't be bought or sold. The commodification of our values and relationships has seriously eroded what we all know to be the essential values for healthy balanced living. Noam Chomsky pointed out that we can "manufacture consent" for any number of values.

The technological distortion of our values can be insidious. Some studies report that 80 percent of communication of young people is by faceless texting. Not only are visual cues lost, but intimacy and extended dialogues are lost as well. The cultural assault on Humanist values is powerful. We are remarkably blind to how all our decisions about values are determined by our immersion in modern culture.

The challenge of freely choosing our values occurs in other ways as well. The evolutionary evolved pleasure circuit in the old limbic brain helped us survive and reproduce without conscious reasoning. We naturally and non-rationally have a visceral urge to eat and have sex. An addiction highjacks the old brain's "pleasure circuit" and wrongly tells us that, for survival, we need to continue the addictive behavior. Its subconscious message is so strong that all our other values are drowned out with the urge to use the addictive substance. It becomes the heavily addicted mind's one and only high value.

People ask why someone would give up all their other values such as health, self-esteem, family, money, safety, and emotional balance in order to keep the addictive behavior going. The answer is simple. The brain subconsciously thinks it will die if it doesn't get the addictive substance. Therefore all other values are secondary to the primal urge for survival.

Even if we can freely choose our values, are there really higher values? There certainly are. Aristotle spoke of the Greek word *eudaimonia*, which generally has been translated as happiness or good spirits, but recent scholars translate more as "flourishing." Flourishing moves our values beyond mere sensual gratification to an appreciation of those values that are elevating to human character.

Consider the movie *The Matrix*, where the heroes choose not to live in a computer-generated world of pure bliss within the Matrix, but choose a mortal life as an autonomous, freely choosing human being. If we put aside all the negative real-world consequences of using heroin, we can see that it provides blissful short term happiness. Yet those who become addicted hate being caught in its unreality, despite the overwhelming short term happiness they achieve while high. Happiness isn't all we want. We crave self-determination, freedom, autonomy, reality and, most important, an authentic life, and will put aside our own immediate happiness for these values. At times, we will even die for freedom, justice, strangers, and the greater good of humanity.

We value something greater than mere visceral pleasure or happiness. We want and value truth, reality and all the values that transcend mere pleasure. We want our autonomy. We want to flourish.

Our values are relative, but they are not arbitrary. They have an objective basis. We are born into a very certain world, with cause and effect relationships, from an evolutionary past that imposes values on us that sustain us and help us flourish. What matters to us is a mixture of necessity, internal drives, and choice. If we were in a different universe, compassion, reason, art, justice and love might not appear or be of value. But we are here, and so are our values. Our highest values, like the physical universe, are emergent properties, not just relative, not merely a reductive property of interacting atoms. These values emerge from who we are and what helps us flourish.

Values emerge like flowers from particular soils in the universe, our earth, our culture, and in our own freedom to choose. Each of us will hold some very high values across the spectrum of time and culture; others will have other values more localized to our time and place, and still other values unique only to ourselves. What matters, what we value, is what emerges out of all of it. That being said, however, a great number of values are universal across cultures.

Some have said Humanism is not a set of beliefs, but a set of values we hold dear and that underlie our life stance. Some of the best of the emergent values we hold to are freedom, intelligence, love, truth, reason, open-mindedness, happiness, tolerance, compassion, sex, responsibility, justice, hope, and art. All of these help us flourish.

We carry the torch of the Enlightenment, which was built on a three-legged stool of these particular values: freedom, reason, and tolerance. The tolerance leg acknowledges that there is no one right way to live our lives, no single universal set of values and purposes for all of us, no single meaning to be grasped by all, and no single grand narrative to guide us.

Is there anything we humans value that doesn't have a downside? I don't think so. Since the Enlightenment, nontheists have sought nonreligious, rational answers to our unending quest for how to live our lives, so this becomes quite important. One of the twentieth century's greatest philosophers, Isaiah Berlin, gave us some crucial insights into this quest.

Berlin popularized the notion of pluralism. He saw, as John Gray put it, a "value-pluralism, that ultimate human values are objective, but irreducibly diverse, that they are conflicting and often uncombinable, and when they do come into conflict with one another they are incommensurable; that is, they are not comparable by any rational measure." Further, "The idea of a perfect society in which all genuine ideals and goods are achieved is not merely utopian; it is incoherent. Political life, like moral life, abounds in radical choice between rival goods and evils, where reason leaves us in the lurch and whatever is done involves loss and sometimes tragedy. Berlin's is a tragic liberalism of unavoidable conflict and irreparable loss among inherently rivalrous values."

Berlin saw human diversity as a rational outcome and said we don't need, nor should we expect to find, a single rational way to live our lives. While science and reason can help us in understanding the world and may help in making decisions about potential outcomes, they nevertheless cannot provide certain grounding for living our lives as individuals or as a society. There are indeed many high values, but none of them provide the ultimate answer.

We all have multiple needs and values. To start with only one as the ultimate first principle is simplistic and irrational. As the journalist H. L. Mencken said, "There is always a well-known solution to every human problem—neat, plausible, and wrong."

A mature understanding of life, ethics, and politics demands that we often have to compromise some of our most cherished principles. This is necessary because many times our values will be in radical conflict in the decisions we make. An ethical life is a balancing act, tragically choosing between tradeoffs with necessary gains and losses, all with the objective of increasing our welfare and minimizing suffering. Idolatry, using any single-minded grand scheme to solve the problems of the world, can be as dangerous in its certainty as any religion.

Some real-world examples illustrate how far off track ideology can take us—in other words, taking one high ideal and elevating it over all others, leading to insidious results. Communists built a secular god of economic justice that consumed and subsumed all other values, including freedom. More than thirty million died in Stalinist Russia for an ideology of economic justice.

Libertarians, on the other hand, have elevated a secular god of radical freedom over all others. Forty-five thousand people died last year for lack of medical care in the United States because of an ideology of freedom that ignored all pragmatic and compassionate arguments. In fact, we have many high values. Freedom and economic justice are indeed part of my high values, but only two of them. I also value love, compassion, joy, tolerance, nature, justice, democracy, a baby's laugh, and butterflies. I value these not because they are rationally "true," but because of what works and out of my own deep-felt emotional passion.

The Communist god of economic justice leads to oppression in the name of compassionate responsibility. The Libertarian god of freedom can be transformed into license—a lack of civility, compassion, responsibility and social justice. A simplistic political/economic theory based on hardened "principles" is very similar to Christian ethical theory built on normative principles called the Ten Commandments. These rigid belief systems are easy, utopian, simplistic, and dangerously wrong. The word utopia literally means "nowhere."

Ideology raises admittedly great values such as economic justice and freedom as secular "gods" over all other values. The arguments for these belief systems are fully rational if one accepts their single-value premise. Ultimately, ideology kills. We all have multiple needs and values and to start with only one as the *summum bonum* is simple-minded, irrational and non-empirical. This reduction of values points in the direction of totalitarianism. Life is simply too complex to fit into such tidy boxes. It is the wise person who grows out of rationalistic simplicity to a more encompassing, and yes, harder Humanism. Building an ethical system based on ideology is surely easy, but wrong if we end up putting ideology ahead of people. As a Humanist, I prefer to put people and results ahead of ideology. That means that sometimes some of our cherished principles will be compromised. That is how it should be, because sometimes, rationally, our highest values will be in conflict. We will always find we are trying to balance rights and responsibility, autonomy and social order, security and freedom.

When our lives are caught in the certainty of a single-minded rationalism, it feels as comforting as belief in God. In actuality, it is a crypt of the mind. Its stone-like edifice rejects real critical thinking and evidence of outcomes. It allows only narrow pathways of thought that are based on the original premises. Can we uncover our own ideologies? Ask yourself, "What are the secular idols that are the touchstones in my own life?" What are the values you choose to elevate over all others? Accordingly, what are the values you simply ignore? In effect, what great Humanistic values have become toxic for you? What value has become poisonous to the ultimate good life we are trying to achieve? Is it freedom? Is it tolerance? Is it compassion? Is it reason itself? Is it justice? Is it love?

Do we have the courage to face the tradeoffs and losses? As Berlin wrote, "Every choice may entail irreparable loss." Are we wise enough to see not just that we have many high values, but that none is the ultimate answer? Can we see that all have the potential for cancerous growth?

We mortals long for simplicity; we long for certainty; we long for a clear path to follow that will guide us to the good life. The sweet surrender of letting ourselves embrace a simple path for life's grand questions, one that doesn't require ambivalence or doubt, has always been alluring. It relieves us of anxieties or ambiguities. Self-righteous certainty follows; it is a heady brew. But it is a dangerous lie.

This awareness is at once alarming and exasperating. But it is also the beginning of hope for a realization that

sets our life on a better course. That is guided by humility, irony and dialogue and lets us see everything we do
as having tradeoffs. Maybe we need to therapeutically
laugh at ourselves at bit more when we get too cocksure
of ourselves, since life does not provide us with a clear
rulebook. Discard certainty in both facts and values! Joyously embrace ambiguity! But this does not mean we need
be paralyzed in determining and making decisions on
what is important and in committing ourselves to those
pathways. Most decisions are pretty obvious; we land on
them easily, not torn by ambiguity.

It is easy to become completely cynical about values
and meaning when one considers many grim realities.
These include the problems of meaning in a meaningless
universe, the insidious power of a dominating culture,
the likelihood that we are choosing our values out of
subconscious drives for power and control, and our nasty
habit of rationalizing our own prejudices. Still, there is no
question that our values are emergent priorities, arising
from our lives, that have a real objective bearing on who
we are and who we will be.

Paul Kurtz addresses our Humanist values this way.
"We are interested in cognitive and ethical questions, in
achieving, especially at the present juncture, a cultural
renaissance or cultural reformation. We offer a distinctive
set of intellectual and normative values. We emphasize the
importance of reason and critical thinking, and we wish to
use these methods in order to reformulate and refashion
our values, and to raise the quality of taste and the level
of appreciation in society. Humanism is life-affirming; it
is positive and constructive. If applied, it would enable
us to reform human culture by transcending the ancient

religious, racial, ethnic, and ideological dogmas of the past that so adversely affect human civilization in the present. We thus call for a reaffirmation of the highest values of which humans are capable."

Humanism asks us to search for and commit ourselves to our highest ideals, our noblest sentiments, our greatest values, and what civilization and science say matters most. Choosing our values affects real people with real lives in real ways. Nothing is relative about that. The universe may not have transcendent values, but higher values do exist, which make all our lives better. These real values motivate us beyond our own petty circumstances to experience a larger reality. That movement lets us achieve a unity of purpose with others. Humanism attempts to build a whole life stance around those highest values and ideals. In the next chapter, we will explore how our values affect our ethical viewpoint.

8

Ethics

"Man is like a tree, with the mighty trunk of intellect, the spreading branches of imagination, and the roots of the lower instincts that bind him to the earth. The moral life, however, is the fruit he bears; in it his true nature is revealed. It is the prerogative of man that he need not blindly follow the law of his natural being, but is himself the author of a higher moral law, and creates it even in acting it out."

– Felix Adler (1851-1933)

How should we live our lives? Much of ethics amounts to answering the question of how much we should do for ourselves as opposed to how much we should be doing for others. Where is the balance point? What follows is a discussion of failed theories and, at first, may seem a complicated waste of time. But I assure you that a discussion of these theories points toward better understanding of how to avoid some pitfalls while building a better secular ethic.

Fundamentally, Humanism is not just humanitarianism or just being Humanistic, that is, being human centered. Humanism is a particular ethical viewpoint.

Traditionally in ethics we must first address the problem of getting from facts in the world to what we should actually do. It is sometimes called the is/ought divide and is in fact a deep, unbridgeable chasm. It is the natural separation of the facts from our values. Logically I can't just say that because cursing someone makes them feel bad is a reason that I should not do it. We truly can't logically connect the chasm from the "is" of something to saying we "ought" to do something. But maybe we can "jump" over that gap.

Pragmatically, if we decide on a goal or goals, then we can legitimately say the facts of the matter can inform us how to best to achieve those goals. The facts tell us the best possible paths if we want to successfully determine what we ought to do. Prescriptivism is just common-sense ethical problem solving.

The ultimate ethical goal for Humanists is the betterment and flourishing of human and global welfare and the mitigating of suffering. That goal is what we jump to over the chasm of is/ought. How we do that is where it gets complicated.

Ultimately we will find that any secular ethical system worth having will be inherently messy, inherently lacking a simple formula, and inherently ambiguous. It will challenge all our capabilities. If it were simple it would be wrong. Ethical systems and, more important, our actual moral behavior exposes our real values. I, like many of you, am terrible at talking about ethics because I am bound up in shame about my own considerable moral lapses. Still, I have sought redemption in both understanding morality and dealing with my own personal demons. I have tried to live a better life. I have seen many for whom a moral life comes as easily as smiling. I greatly admire these people, whom we have all met at one time and place or another. They seem incapable of immorality. Living a life of sincere empathy and moral behavior, they serve as important role models.

Those with a natural morality may have their hearts in the right place, but can still be led astray by ideology. One only need look at the history of the Holocaust and of Stalinist Russia when millions of civilized people were led to commit genocide. Or consider events today when many essentially good people kill in the name of religion. As the Nobel-winning physicist and 2002 Humanist of the Year Steven Weinberg said, "Religion is an insult to human dignity. With or without it, you would have good people doing good things and evil people doing evil things. But for good people to do evil things, that takes religion."

While ethical theory can provide a conceptual framework, we must also look how we actually act morally. How are so many naturally inclined to good behavior and yet most of us struggle? And how is it that around one percent of us are natural sociopaths?

The Enlightenment brought hopes that rationality could provide a firm foundation for secular ethics to replace the Judeo-Christian ethic. We have seen many attempts to solve that question, and consistent failures. Maybe you thought there was a "right" or "wrong" ethical theory to live by. We will examine some of these attempts, as each has exposed some new truth about who we are and what our ethical compass tells us. It will be helpful if we approach this study from several viewpoints to get a multi-dimensional picture.

One conceptual framework is to see that ethical theories generally fall into two categories: based on either the rules or the consequences. Most ethical systems involve focusing on one or the other. Sometimes we justify an ethical decision using both the act (or rules) and the consequences, but ultimately one argument or the other prevails. Another way to describe the alternatives is the difference between the right and the good, the use of first principles, and conversely a focus on the projected outcomes. Each actually means something a little different, but for our purposes here we can look at them interchangeably.

> Rules or act → Consequences
> Right → Good
> First principles → Projected outcome

The Ten Commandments is an example of an ethical framework based on acts or a set of rules. The doctor's credo of "First, do no harm" is an example of a consequentialist, good-based ethical standard for decision making. While each results in ethical systems that seem complete and beautiful in theory, they are logically incompatible. Both ethical theories cannot be true, because they conflict with each other in principle and in practice. Let's look at each of these ethical systems in more detail.

Rule/act-based ethical systems

The Enlightenment philosopher Immanuel Kant was the first to provide a secular right-based, rule-based ethics. He formulated the idea that we find absolute, unconditional rules by what he calls the categorical imperative. Kant argued that we should make ethical decisions based only on universal, non-subjective first principles, which are found through rational means. To be an ethically valid first principle, it must be universally valid. He gave the following formula for determining those rules:

"Act only according to that maxim whereby you can, at the same time, will that it should become a universal law."

In Kant's view, moral duty is the first ethical principle. Adhering to hard and fast universal rules is what is important, not the consequences of an action. Of course we all admire people who are "principled," but Kant allowed no wiggle room to avoid rigidly sticking to the principles.

The Ten Commandments are the most well-known rule based ethical system coming from the Old Testament. But the Jewish tradition holds that a good Jew must actually observe 613 mitzvot or commandments.

Hard and fast rules can present problems, though. During World War II in thousands of real life instances people hid Jews and were interrogated by the Nazis. If they had obeyed sacred rules against lying, they would have been obligated to tell the truth, sending the Jews to their deaths. This is a horrible outcome that shows the problems with slavishly sticking to inflexible rules. Also, if the question is asked about what is the grounding for a categorical imperative rule, we know from the previous chapter on knowledge that we have no ultimate, certain foundations for our beliefs.

Consider this. Can we think of any rule that doesn't require an exception? During World War II I would have lied if the Nazis asked if I was hiding a Jew in my home.

You probably would have, too. As a last resort, I am willing to kill someone in self-defense if my own life is in jeopardy. How am I to choose between my highest moral rules if they are in conflict? As we learned in the chapter on values, our highest values are many times in radical conflict and we have no clear choice. So it is we find with ethical rules, which often will be in radical, irresolvable conflict. The reality is that sometimes we may have to choose between the lesser of two evils. Sometimes deciding the answer is simple; at other times it is not and we are conflicted.

As we also saw in the early chapter on values, it is so easy to rationalize our behavior using reason as a weapon, justifying our ethical system by choosing one value over all the others. It seems so logical and it is so dangerous, because we can rationalize rules that merely confirm our prejudices.

There are other rights-based ethical systems, the most notable being the system developed by the social contract theorist John Rawls. He posited an "original" position moral theory with the following premises derived from questioning how we should act toward each other if we didn't know where we were born and to who and what advantages and disadvantages we may have:

1. Each person is to have an equal right to the most extensive basic liberty compatible with a similar liberty for others.
2. Social and economic inequalities are to be arranged so that:

a. They are to be of the greatest benefit to the least-advantaged members of society (the difference principle).

b. Offices and positions must be open to everyone under conditions of fair equality of opportunity.

He argues these premises because, "No one knows his place in society, his class position or social status, nor does anyone know his fortune in the distribution of natural assets and abilities, his intelligence, strength, and the like. I shall even assume that the parties do not know their conceptions of the good or their special psychological propensities. The principles of justice are chosen behind a veil of ignorance. ... They are the principles that rational and free persons concerned to further their own interests would accept in an initial position of equality as defining the fundamentals of the terms of their association."

Again we are faced with asking why an original position premise should be the one we are primarily concerned about. Why should social concerns override those of individual aspirations? Still, even if this theory is flawed, there seems to be something of value in asking the original position question of ourselves. It brings awareness and helps us temper the arrogance of our own privileged position.

Lastly, let's give an example that we all know and generally accept as a fundamental moral principle, the Golden Rule. For good reason, it is found in both its positive and negative forms throughout all cultures. It works, as an easily remembered rule that reminds us to be empathetic. Regardless of how valuable it appears as a day-to-day moral touchstone, even the Golden Rule can support behavior we could all find disturbing.

In many reported instances in Muslim societies, people have been burned, stoned, and murdered by their own families for disobeying Islamic law. One case in Afghanistan involved a young couple whose family discovered they had met in secret without chaperones. For this disgrace to family honor, they were to be stoned by the family. To compound the horror, the children agreed that they probably should be stoned, but asked for compassion. If you asked them if the parents were adhering to the sound moral principle of the Golden Rule, they would agree and indeed they would see it as their duty to stone another member of their family in the same situation. Even the great Golden Rule can be seen as merely reflecting and supporting the societal norms, even when those norms are monstrous abuses of human dignity.

These examples tell us that act-based or rule-based ethics has deep problems: for every rule there are exceptions, problems in ungrounded foundations, problems in those foundations being culturally biased, problems with certain values dominating others and reflecting our prejudices, problems in placing ideology over what actually happens in our lives, and a disconnect from morality as a lived virtue.

Yet there is something important in having simple rules of behavior to guide us, even if they may conflict. These are called "heuristics." The Golden Rule should be honored, as it still works most of the time in our personal lives. We all live with these simple rules: don't lie, don't cheat, don't hurt people, be kind, be compassionate. As a matter of practicality we seem to need simple, easily remembered guideposts, if not for personal behavior, then at least for societal legal systems. Legal systems are primarily rule based, but because juries and judges have some discretion, the systems have some flexibility.

Good-based / consequentialist systems of ethics

The other great ethical system is based on the consequences of our actions and striving for the "good." Consequentialist ethics tells us to dispense with rational rules with all their flaws, and look at what actually happens to help or hurt people. With no transcendent purpose or values in the universe, we are the meaning makers, the seat of where values are determined, so it would seem that only our fulfillment of meaning and values carries any weight. Usually the end goal is framed something like "human and global welfare."

One form of consequentialism resembles act-based ethics, called Rule-based utilitarianism. It posits that we should develop evolving, flexible rules to guide our acts, but to obtain those from experience about what works for the overall welfare, not follow rigid rational rules.

The best-known type of consequentialism is utilitarianism, where one tries to maximize the total benefits and reduce the total suffering. One decides what to do depending on the best likely outcome. Originally this moral theory would only apply to humans, but later theorists enjoined us to consider all sentient beings and even all of nature. Intrinsic value is now considered given for all forms of life and nature, whether sentient or not.

Consequentialism and its subset utilitarianism are adaptive to the situation and yield multiple and even conflicting results. Most people, and certainly the secular, hold to some form of consequentialism, but there are problems to consider before embracing it too easily.

First of all, many consider some forms of consequentialism unrealistic. That is because you would need to be willing to personally sacrifice everything in order to pursue the most beneficial course of action for the greater good. Remembering that if the ultimate question of morality is to discover how much to do for others vs. oneself, the balance is highly skewed toward society. This ethical system idealistically ignores our instinctual selfishness and acts as if those impulses can be ignored or entirely overcome.

A deeper problem, though, is one that many ethicists think is illuminated in the fictional account by Ursula LeGuin, *The Ones Who Walk Away from Omelas*. Omelas is a shimmering city of unbelievable happiness and delight. Citizens blissfully live, sharing communal resources, and are intelligent, sophisticated, and cultured. It is a city free of disease, famine, crime and want. Omelas has no kings, soldiers, priests, or slaves. Peace and contentment fill everyone's heart.

But the city has a dark secret. "The city has a guarantee of happiness; it has struck a bargain, although how and with whom it is not clear. The bargain is this: In a room under the city is a stunted, frightened, half-starved child, and everyone over adolescence in Omelas knows that the child is there. ... In a basement under one of the beautiful public buildings of Omelas, or perhaps in the cellar of one of its spacious private homes, there is a room. It has one locked door, and no window."

The room is a mere broom closet with a dirt floor, a mop and a bucket. The child is afraid of the mop. Sometimes someone comes to open the locked door to leave a little food and water, but they kick the child.

"The people at the door never say anything, but the child, who has not always lived in the tool room, and can remember sunlight and its mother's voice, sometimes speaks. 'I will be good,' it says. 'Please let me out. I will be good!' They never answer. The child used to scream for help at night, and cry a good deal, but now it only makes a kind of whining, 'eh-haa, eh-haa,' and it speaks less and less often. It is so thin there are no calves to its legs; its belly protrudes; it lives on a half-bowl of corn meal and grease a day. It is naked. Its buttocks and thighs are a mass of festered sores, as it sits in its own excrement continually."

"They all know it is there, all the people of Omelas. Some of them have come to see it, others are content merely to know it is there. They all know that it has to be there. Some of them understand why, and some do not, but they all understand that their happiness, the beauty of their city, the tenderness of their friendships, the health of their children, the wisdom of their scholars, the skill of their makers, even the abundance of their harvest and the kindly weathers of their skies, depend wholly on this child's abominable misery."

"They would like to do something for the child. But there is nothing they can do. If the child were brought up into the sunlight out of that vile place, if it were cleaned and fed and comforted, that would be a good thing, indeed; but if it were done, in that day and hour all the prosperity and beauty and delight of Omelas would wither and be destroyed. Those are the terms. To exchange all the goodness and grace of every life in Omelas for that single, small improvement: to throw away the happiness of thousands for the chance of the happiness of one: that would be to let guilt within the walls indeed."

I hope you are touched by this story and find something viscerally horrifying regarding human dignity, freedom, human rights, compassion, and a monstrous use of "the ends justifying the means." It tells us that pure utilitarianism can justify huge abuses, especially to minorities, in the name of the greater good. The "end" can justify horrible means if we don't stand up for high moral principles. One can even make a parallel example concerning impoverished children today who remain "invisible" while we reward a few at the expense of those who have not participated in our modern-day Omelas.

Now let's step back a moment before we too readily decide to walk away from Omelas. The Utilitarian Peter Singer told me he would leave Omelas. But what if the city had two billion inhabitants? How about two million? How about two hundred? How about only twenty? Possibly your answer might vary with the population and its total effects. This is called situational ethics and the ethical lines aren't clear, are they? Each situation demands a new look without simple formulas. It illustrates the ambiguity inherent in many, but certainly not all of our ethical decisions.

The story of Omelas does teach us the danger, as the saying goes, that if we lose compassion we can wind up doing anything. If we make compassion a vice, we probably will. We can also flip it around and say that if we make compassion a secular god, the good of the whole can be decreased, because freeloaders and cheats will take advantage. Much of the liberal-conservative political divide can be seen in finding the balance point between compassion and providing incentives for personal responsibility.

Both consequentialism and act-based ethics have serious problems. Something seems to be so seductively, rationally true about both, but when we look closely we see that each has unacceptable conflicting fault lines, if we think either has the complete answer.

Judge a moral system, a political system, an economic system, or a person, not by their system's piety and consistency, but what happens in real people's lives to ennoble them or degrade them. As the Bible says, "By their fruits you shall know them."

Virtue ethics

More recent is the act-based ethical position of Alasdair MacIntyre's virtue ethics. He argues that since all attempts at rationalistic ethical systems stemming from the Enlightenment have failed, we should look back to the ancient Greeks and in particular to Aristotle. He did not use formalized rules for ethical decisions, but looked to a person's character to inform good moral decisions. A good person naturally acts correctly, based not on following formal rules about either acts or consequences, but on good character and balanced moral virtues. Those include generosity, courage, kindness, loyalty, honesty, politeness, and benevolence.

This ethical system acknowledges that our sentiments are more important than reason and that these can be transmitted to others. There is an intuitional aspect to deciding between ethical dilemmas, virtue ethics holds, and people of virtuous character are best suited to decide.

Its attraction is its focus on character and how morality is lived out in real life, but it doesn't propose any ideas to guide us in decision-making, using either rules or consequences. Some argue that this ethical system is inherently conservative, standing for what is moral in the dominant culture. More important, it does not tell us what sorts of actions are morally good and which ones are not. Instead, it focuses on what character virtues are needed to become a good person. Undoubtedly, people of good character show us by their actions how to live a moral life, not by just giving abstract rational rules and making us question what virtues are worth having.

The researcher Carol Gilligan and the philosopher Nel Noddings point us specifically toward a virtue ethic of care and concern. Noddings argues that caring, "rooted in receptivity, relatedness, and responsiveness" is a more fundamental approach to ethics. All of this gets more complicated in light of recent studies that have found that one can have compassion but not empathy, or conversely, empathy and not compassion. The psychologist Paul Bloom even argues that empathy can get in the way of making rational compassionate choices. Also we will find later that the psychology professor Jonathan Haidt's more recent research provides a more thorough understanding of our moral psychology; it takes caring into consideration along with other moral drives.

Moral pluralism

Well, we've punctured a few ethical theory balloons so far. Actually, we could name and debunk dozens of ethical theories, but those we have talked about so far are the main ones. The bottom line is that after a few centuries of searching, no "grand" secular theory has stood up as coherent, well grounded, complete, and without major problems.

Rule-based ethics like the Ten Commandments and Kantian ethics have problems in that nothing firmly grounds them; there are always exceptions, and the rules often conflict with each other. Consequentialist ethics can have problems with justice and protection of minorities; also, the end consequences are plural and in general conflict with each other. Some, such as the neuroscientist and philosopher Sam Harris, propose that science can tell us the correct decisions. But that still leaves us deciding consequences to choose; and the sheer complexities of daily moral decision-making make detailed analysis impractical. This is not to say science cannot tell us a great deal. It can be useful to inform us about the likely projected outcomes. Virtue and care ethics leaves us with no firm grounding to deal with ethical dilemmas and with no guide for action. Some, like those in the Vienna Circle of philosophers, sometimes called logical positivists, said all ethical statements are meaningless, merely asking for approval or disapproval. This idea is sometimes disparagingly known as the "Boo/Hooray" theory. Some relativists say ethics is all just a culturally based phenomenon. Confused?

Don't despair, as there are some answers.

Consider this thought experiment. Suppose there is a forested planet where sentient beings live, with markedly different behavior patterns from our own. Suppose they are toxic in contact with each other except for one day each five years. That one day is a breeding season when they mate, and then after mating one eats the other for nourishment, somewhat like the praying mantis and some spiders do. The young are produced by live birth, but will not survive without the extra nourishment of the mate's body being eaten. They live in a very cultured society with art and music being of high value. Some believe these values were biologically driven to lure an unsuspecting mate. Still, communication among this species is very limited. Art is created and music is played as predatory lures left in the forest.

In such a world, a biological imperative resulted in the species being remarkably solitary, independent, manipulative and non-societal, where music, art, murder and cannibalism are required for reproduction. Their lack of a cooperative society, their values and ethical standards emerged out of their unique situation or they would not exist.

In this hypothetical example we can see how ethics is an emergent property, but with very objective standards that emerge out of a meaningless universe. As with values, ethics are relative, but not arbitrary. The universe does not care a hoot what your ethics are, but in the constraints of a real world that is not relative, driven by cause and effect, certain patterns of behaviors emerge because they work well for the species within that environment.

In our own case, we are social animals driven by conflicting needs for both cooperation and selfishness. For most of our history we have been constrained by scarce resources, so gathering precious food and water has weighed heavily on who we are. When I hear lofty nonsensical arguments that ethics are totally relative, I want to ask those who say this to prove their point: either by taking goods away from someone or hurting them in any culture. Our actions have real consequences. Ethical behavior may be relative in the universe, but its effects are very real here and now on our earth. There can be huge ethical differences between various cultures, but the underlying boundaries are given to us not by God or the universe, but by our specific environment.

Where does morality come from?

Many people devoted to religion would say morals come from God. But ask them this: "If they stopped believing today, would they live their lives any differently?" They will generally agree that they wouldn't change anything. The Christian Bible and the Koran are filled with many things most of us would say are immoral, such as genocide, slavery, homophobia, human sacrifices, subjugation of women, etc., so we know most people do not follow the dictates of their religious tradition.

Morality comes from human needs and interests. Digging deeper, morality stems from a combination of genetic drives, reason, compassion, human agency, social influences, and self-interest. Let's look at these bio-psycho-social origins in more detail.

There is a whole academic discipline called evolutionary ethics that examines morality as an adaptive trait that evolved for us to get along in small hunter-gatherer tribes. We are predisposed towards certain behaviors. If you were kicked out of the tribe because of lying, cheating, fighting with others or not doing your share of the work, you were as good as dead. Alone on the African savanna, you didn't last very long and your genes were not passed along. Those who were inclined to work together cooperatively were more likely to survive and to have more children.

Another genetic drive comes from what is called kin selection. If one furthers the survival of one's close relatives, even at a cost to your own survival and reproduction, it indirectly furthers the reproduction of your genes. Those that sacrifice their own lives to save their children in effect perpetuate their own genes.

Reciprocal altruism is another driver for moral concerns. If you are in a small tribe and have food when others don't, it pays you to give some to others; later on you may need some when you don't have any. Animals exhibit this quid pro quo behavior all the time. Vampire bats are a good example because they can only live for a few days without food. If they have a poor night's hunting, other bats will feed them some of their coagulated blood and they in turn will do the same later on. They couldn't survive otherwise. Scratching someone else's back with expectations of them returning the favor is one of the backbones of societal cohesion and survival.

Another moral genetic drive derives from reputational trust. People learn to respect those who exhibit altruism and are trustworthy. People do better in their tribes if they are known as people of character. Moral virtue pays.

We must be motivated to act on what we think leads to the good life. Studies by Antonio R. Damasio, an American neuroscientist, have shown that reason and cognition are not the primary sources of moral decisions. By studying patients with damaged ventromedial connections from the emotional center in the midbrain to the cognitive centers in the neocortex, he found that the primary decision-maker for ethical choices resides in the emotional, subconscious regions. The "I" of the "authentic self" is more hidden from view than we realized. The so-called "free will" is not so free. This does not mean reason is not an important voice in the decision-making process, but we can never underestimate the power of our emotions. This is why it seems important to increase both our rational and our emotional intelligence. It is why consciousness-raising and intentionally increasing our empathy and compassion are important.

What these findings say is that our subconscious emotional voices can overwhelm all sense of rational analysis. This can also be seen in recent studies by Jonathan Haidt.

Haidt has found that we have six main instinctual moral foundations, which is true across cultures:

1. Care/harm for others, protecting them from harm.
2. Fairness/cheating, justice, treating others in proportion to their actions. (He has also referred to this dimension as proportionality.)
3. Liberty/oppression, characterizes judgments in terms of whether subjects are tyrannized.
4. Loyalty/betrayal to your group, family, nation. (He has also referred to this dimension as ingroup.)
5. Authority/subversion for tradition and legitimate authority. (He has also connected this foundation to a notion of respect.)
6. Sanctity/degradation, avoiding disgusting things, foods, actions. (He has also referred to this as Purity.)

While all of us have all these traits, he and others have found, interestingly, that liberals tend to focus on the first three while conservatives tend to place greater emphasis on the last three. This is true even across many cultures. It is important to point out that these instinctual psychological traits are what influences us, but they do not tell us philosophically what we should do. They are an example of the "is", the facts, but not the "oughts." There is an instinctual bias built into these moral foundations, but we don't know from these impulses alone what we should or shouldn't do.

Reason itself does have a role in moral behavior. Game theory has studied human behavior in the famous "prisoner's dilemma" and hundreds of variants. They surprisingly found that cooperative strategies were the most successful in competitive computer games beginning with one called "tit for tat." While later studies have shown some limitations, it appears that in many cases cooperation works better in the long term than cutthroat competition.

Cultural influences also greatly affect our moral outlook. We can find cultures that have just the opposite of any moral outlook we may hold dear. Some cultures hold stealing and violence in esteem.

The famous book by Colin Turnbull, *The Mountain People*, documented the plight of a normal African tribe, the Ik, who after being relocated suffered incredible famine. As Claude Steiner said, "After a couple of generations of starvation conditions, the Ik, originally a cooperative, child-loving tribe, became a group of selfish, cruel people who don't trust or help anybody. They would desert children at an early age." Turnbull relates a story that after abandoning a baby to be eaten by wild animals, the tribesmen hunted and ate the animals. Our cultural/environmental conditions can radically change our morality. Some point out that our modern alienated society creates more psychopaths.

How did prewar Germany, one of the most cultured
societies, descend to the horrors of the Holocaust? As
mentioned earlier, if there is any lesson from the Holocaust
it seems that a civilization can easily slip into barbarism.
Early Humanists and science in general saw human nature as completely moldable; a *tabula rasa* or blank slate
that culture impressed itself upon. Human beings were
viewed as essentially good. After the Holocaust there
could be no doubt that we have the seeds for both great
good or great evil.

Our morality also arises from necessity. The consequences of a jail sentence for violence or theft keeps us
in line.

So we find there are many reasons for our ethical behavior. Our evolution gives us instincts toward morality; it is
rational to do so; we learn how to be moral from society;
it is of practical help to us; and there are consequences
if don't act well. That is why religious persons who give
up God are unlikely to change their moral behavior. They
have already learned a set of moral behaviors.

Ethical dilemmas

As I have suggested, one of the keys to understanding
ethics is to get rid of any idea of a grand, all-encompassing
ethical theory. We've tried over and over and failed to
create one. Further, it is crucial to understand that ethical
dilemmas abound in daily life. Making most of our ethical
decisions is pretty easy, but some dilemmas can present
problems. Ethical dilemmas are situations in which neither
of two or more options resolves the situation without in-

fringing on some essential ethical position. We face three primary reasons for being cursed with moral dilemmas.

Philosophical reasons – Often we are torn between whether our decision should be based on the rules or on the consequences. Also, we have seen that all ethical theories have major problems. Still, each seems to have some measure of truth, some valuable but flawed moral basis. We are torn between our conflicting ethical foundations.

Reasons of value – Isaiah Berlin's concept that we have multiple high values that are in radical conflict directly affects ethics. Our morals reflect our values. We may place a high value on love, but in an abusive relationship, love can blind us. We may value freedom and property rights, but that can lead to total license to cut down a last stand of redwoods and a lack of responsibility to society. As Berlin points out, there are always downsides and tradeoffs to any of our values and hence our moral decisions.

Neuropsychological reasons – We know now that much of what goes on in the brain happens in the subconscious. Mental activity is a mixture of the bio-psycho-social. While we may have noble thoughts and ideals of morality, we have to deal with the reality that no matter how well we try, we can never completely overcome what happens hidden from our view. As humanist Bruce S. Springsteen said, "As restless as we can be, we are mentally static beasts, not so far from mindless instinct, reflex, and dogged habit as we flatter ourselves."

If moral dilemmas permeate all our ethical decisions and there are no grand ethical theories, how can we, as Socrates put it, know how to live?

How can we make moral decisions?

The political scientist James Q. Wilson told us, "Moral sense is natural." Compassion is our natural empathy, reinforced by our upbringing. We are interdependent and interconnected social creatures who want to get along. We suffer shame and embarrassment.

Here is how we can make moral decisions. First, one needs overall goals. Originally Humanism looked primarily at human welfare. As our knowledge grew, we learned that much of the difference between us and other animals is in degree, not kind. We learned that the degree of sentience in animals is greater than we thought. We are only beginning to understand animals' degree of consciousness. Still, it appears that humans do have some unique abilities in language and a heightened sense of self-awareness. We don't need to descend to speciesism to say that as far as we know, humans are the only beings capable of significant moral action. If it's going to happen, it's up to us.

Ultimately each of us has multiple ethical goals. Building an ethical framework is not like solving a mathematical equation. Building a morality is more like painting a picture with different colors and hues, or assembling a collage of various pieces. We have to use all the "tools" in our garage. The simplest way I can explain our Humanist ethical goal is this: *We try to enhance the welfare or flourishing of all of humanity and the biosphere we are part of.* These are the ultimate consequences that matter. Fundamentally humanism promotes consequentialism.

Note that we are caught with multiple end goals. If it sounds difficult to choose between multiple goals, it can be. I may have to choose between myself, my loved ones, humanity at large, and the biosphere, but that's how it is. It's messy. If you are not torn in your loyalties, I suggest you are not looking carefully. Ambiguity is a fundamental fact of life. How we deal with it is crucial.

Some people can't handle ambiguity. Instead, they will latch onto a simplistic ideology. That is how religious fundamentalism and "one-way" thinking secular ideologies are born. Accepting and working through ambiguity, diverse loyalties, and trade-offs seems to be a mark of maturity. Interestingly, studies have shown that liberals can handle ambiguity better than conservatives and children, who tend more toward black-and-white, absolutist thinking.

So if we don't have an overall ethical system to guide us toward our goals through the quagmire of ethical dilemmas, what do we have? The answer appears to be the same as in Chapter 5, on what we know. The best current approach seems to be an ethical pluralism model. We already discussed that Humanism is based on consequential thinking, but we know that is not enough. We need a garage-full of ethical tools.

Because no satisfactory overarching moral theory has been found, we need to base our ethics on what really happens in people's lives, not on abstract ideas. Consequentialism is our first principle—as long as we are careful not to let the ends always justify the means. We require a reasoned combination of the good and the right. This requires that we base our ethical decisions on the consequences of our actions, bearing in mind that we still should use our highest ethical principles—those that are rooted in their proven effectiveness.

Regarding rules and principles: we cannot separate the means from the ends, that is, the act or rules from their consequences. Yet only the ends justify the means. Paradoxically, we still need to inform our consequentialist decisions using tools based on rule/act thinking. These are what have been proven to give the best consequences. These short rules are time-tested for living well as long as we realize they are never perfect and always have exceptions. You can think of consequence- and rule-based principles counterbalancing each other. The irony is that we can't have a good consequentialist ethic unless we adhere to basic moral principles. The bedrock moral principles—don't do violence to others, don't lie, care for those in suffering, each person has equal moral worth, and the Golden Rule—should stand as guiding principles for us. It's just that each isn't enough, can have contradictions, and has limitations.

Here is a summary of Humanist ethics: Our goal?

Our ultimate goal is the betterment and flourishing of human and global welfare and the mitigation of suffering.

Why?

Humanist ethics are based on the fact that only we are responsible for our ethics and that we must determine our own ethical lives. Only we are responsible for our ethics because only we have any control. Morality stems from human agency, reason, compassion, social influences, genetic drives, and self-interest.

How?

Humanist ethics look at the consequences of a decision, at the same time holding to sound moral rules and principles.

Other moral tools?

We are all coequal centers of worth, freedom and authority. We affirm each person's equal worth and dignity. This is prescriptive, not descriptive. We will expand on this in the next chapter.

We develop our best ethical lives from reason, compassion and reflective inquiry. Humanism uses reason in the service of compassion. It is a form of ethical practice.

All universal "oughts," duties and rules that we develop are conditional. All rules and principles may be in conflict with each other, have exceptions, and must be prefaced by, "All things being equal."

There should be a balanced concern for the individual and society. Life is a contest between self-interest and social interest.

Similarly, human welfare is our primary, but not our only concern. There is a tension between human welfare and the rest of the biosphere.

Morality is best looked at situationally. Each situation is different and must be judged accordingly.

Warnings?

Since all ethical decisions are heavily biased by self-interest, a healthy moral skepticism is always required.

The protection of minorities is always a concern with any moral decision.

Many, but not all, of our moral judgments are dilemmas that require us to choose without a clear path between conflicting choices of two or more goods—or evils. All our greatest values are in radical conflict with each other. Even though there is no clear path we are, as the philosopher Jean-Paul Sartre said, "Condemned to choose," sometimes without firm guidance.

People are ends in themselves, Kant said, and never merely a means to someone else's ends.

Moral judgments require using both heart and mind, both reason and compassion.

9

Meaning

"Humanism is the light of my life and the fire in my soul. It is the deep felt conviction, in every fiber of my being, that human love is a power far transcending the relentless, onward rush of our largely deterministic cosmos. All human life must seek a reason for existence within the bounds of an uncaring physical world, and it is love coupled with empathy, democracy, and a commitment to selfless service which undergirds the faith of a Humanist." – Bette Chambers, past president of the American Humanist Association

If we humans are the meaning makers and life has no absolute meaning, does that mean our search for meaning is, well, meaningless? Not so. In fact, we will find the quest and commitment to our highest meanings are crucial to the good life. Most, though not all, people try to find some meaning in life. Meaning signifies what gives each of us purpose or what has significance. For many in the world, life's meaning is merely to survive another day. For many, who have abundance in their lives and little want, life becomes a placid continuum of happiness. They have little reason to search for overriding meanings in life. For others, the search for meaning can become an obsession.

How can we hold meaning while living in a meaning-less universe where nothing we do can prevent inevitable death? The French existentialist Albert Camus had two stories in that regard. In one he challenged us boldly, "There is but one truly serious philosophical problem and that is suicide." His challenge, if we choose to live, is to give up on senseless searches for meaning and transcendence in an absurd world that is devoid of God or any overarching purpose. Camus answered the question of suicide with: "No. It requires revolt."

Camus began his essay *The Myth of Sisyphus* with, "The gods had condemned Sisyphus to ceaselessly rolling a rock to the top of a mountain, whence the stone would fall back of its own weight. They had thought with some reason that there was no more dreadful punishment than futile and hopeless labor." The metaphor vividly describes our own futile and absurd modern lives. Yet Sisyphus finds "silent joy" when, after the rock rolls down, he alone freely makes a decision to go back down and roll the rock back up again. He has, if nothing else, the power and freedom to choose. "This universe henceforth without a master seems to him neither sterile nor futile. The struggle itself toward the heights is enough to fill a man's heart. One must imagine Sisyphus happy."

People have a great range of meanings, but there is some consistency across humanity. The 1967 Humanist of the Year, Abraham Maslow, sought to find out how a normal person functions. (See *Why Was I Born?* by Lyle

Simpson). Plenty of psychological studies have been devoted to abnormal psychology, but Maslow asked what leads to a healthy functioning person. He developed a new approach called humanistic psychology, believing that everyone has a strong desire to realize his or her full potential, to reach a level of "self-actualization." He saw that when persons are in harmony with life, they enjoy "peak experiences" where there is a loss of one's ego, they feel a oneness with all, and experience an elevated, rapturous feeing of consciousness.

Maslow famously theorized that we progress along a hierarchy of needs. We have to satisfy our basic physiological needs of food, water, sleep and sex before we can even think about higher needs. Next, we need to secure our needs for security such as a job, property, health, and physical safety. After that we seek love and belonging, especially from family and friends. Next, we seek self-respect and esteem. Only then can we move to self-actualization and peak experiences, moving out of our own needs and embracing a fuller meaning in other's lives and needs.

Maslow also observed that a fully healthy person has a value set of wholeness, justice, destiny, fairness, self-regulation, complexity, honesty, beauty, goodness, individuality, grace, playfulness, and independence.

Maslow was a unique pioneer. Even though some have contested some of his theory, he appears to have had his hand on essential aspects of how we gain meaning, purpose and happiness.

Carl Rogers, the 1964 Humanist of the Year, said, "This process of the good life is not, I am convinced, a life for the faint-hearted. It involves the stretching and growing of becoming more and more of one's potentialities. It involves *the courage to be.* It means launching oneself fully into the stream of life."

Victor Frankl was an Austrian psychiatrist who suffered through and survived the Nazi concentration camps. He observed in his great book *Man's Search for Meaning* that those who survived invariably stayed alive only because they held onto some transcendent sense of meaning and purpose. Frankl concluded that even in the most horrid, painful, and dehumanized situation we can find potential meaning. He concluded that in a harsh universe all of us require some transcendent meaning to inspire us. He said, notably, "What is to give light must endure burning." To endure suffering we need something within us that gives us meaning beyond ourselves.

Frankl also said, "For the meaning of life differs from man to man, from day to day and from hour to hour. What matters, therefore, is not the meaning of life in general, but rather the specific meaning of a person's life at a given moment."

After his imprisonment and a forced march on icy roads where he almost died, he wrote: "But my mind clung to my wife's image, imagining it with an uncanny acuteness ... A thought transfixed me: for the first time in my life I saw the truth as it is set into song by so many poets, proclaimed as the final wisdom by so many thinkers. The truth—that love is the ultimate and the highest goal to which Man can aspire."

Remember this story when people tell you that without God there is no meaning in life.

Frankl found in interviewing Holocaust survivors that the single most important factor in cultivating the kind of "inner hold" that allowed survival was holding some future goal. He cited Friedrich Nietzsche, who wrote, "He who has a why to live for can bear with almost any how."

Frankl continued, "Ultimately, man should not ask what the meaning of his life is, but rather he must recognize that it is he who is asked. In a word, each man is questioned by life; and he can only answer to life by answering for his own life; to life he can only respond by being responsible."

We do not find the meaning of life alone, but in reflection with one another.

Each of us has to find meanings that sustain us through life's broken times. Ultimate meaning can be God for the theist, but for the Humanist, meaning can spring from a number of sources. Another Holocaust victim, the Nobel Prize-winning Elie Wiesel, wrote the book, *Night*, about his experiences in the Nazi concentration camps. He recounts how his father, though deathly ill, stayed alive for his young son when many others just gave up and died.

Wiesel, like many Holocaust survivors, lost his religious faith amid the horrors of the death camps. He told of being forced to watch the excruciatingly slow hanging of a small boy. One of the other inmates watching the horror whispered, "Where is God? Where is he?" Recalling this, Wiesel said "And from within me, I heard a voice answer: "Where He is? This is where—hanging here from this gallows."

Although Elie Wiesel lost his faith in God, he somehow gained a deeper faith in justice and in each human being's inherent worth and dignity. He became a fierce opponent of the forces that would strip people of their dignity and lives. Of course he is not saying we are actually gods, but rather pointing to where our ultimate loyalties need to lie.

Many say the meaning of life is to find pleasure or happiness. To a large extent this is true. Yet we require something more, much more. Recall that the Greek word *eudaimonia* has been translated as "flourishing" by such scholars as Bernard Williams. If mere pleasure were our ultimate goal in life, think of those who unselfishly chose martyrdom in service of others. Many devote themselves to, and are willing to die for, an ideal larger than themselves.

Joseph Campbell, a student of mythology, said, "I don't believe people are looking for the meaning of life as much as they are looking for the experience of being alive."

Without overarching meaning in our lives, we cannot flourish. We can live, but we will not achieve *eudaimonia* without powerful meanings in our lives. Too many people lead lives of apathy, despair, indifference, and passivity. As mentioned earlier in the chapter on values, we are immersed in a consumerist culture that tells us only marketable goods and services have real value. The result is a distorted sense of what matters. Our culture bombards us with messages that delude us. Critical reasoning and examination of our heart's deepest longings can help us decide what values and ultimate meanings are really important. Many people sleepwalk through life, placing themselves on automatic pilot, unreflective and unaware of their choices. Real wonder can be lost when we don't know what really matters to us.

Victor Frankl saw this in his own time when he said, "Ever more people today have the means to live, but no meaning to live for."

Elie Wiesel said, "Our obligation is to give meaning to life and in doing so to overcome the passive, indifferent life."

So what meanings do we commit ourselves to?

We find meaning in life's immediate joy. As Woody Allen joked, "Sex without love is a meaningless experience, but as far as meaningless experiences go it's pretty damn good."

The philosopher and secular humanist Paul Kurtz insightfully said, "The meaning of life is not to be discovered only after death in some hidden, mysterious realm; on the contrary, it can be found by eating the succulent fruit of the Tree of Life and by living in the here and now as fully and creatively as we can."

I apologize for all these quotations but I think these wise people all have important things to say about where to place our commitments. We can't rationally "prove" they are right, but these voices carry the weight of experience. Of course, we live in a meaningless universe, but the meanings we adopt have real power to shape our futures and those of others. The existentialists talk of the absurdity of life and yet Jean-Paul Sartre saw it this way: not only do we have freedom, we are condemned to it. Often we have no rational way to choose between various alternatives, but we are still bound to choose. Even not choosing involves a choice; choosing apathy and indifference is still a choice.

There is no better statement of the meaning we Humanists have of the world than one attributed to Ralph Waldo Emerson: "The purpose of life is not to be happy. It is to be useful, to be honorable, to be compassionate, to have it make some difference that you have lived and lived well."

Humanists choose to live the fullest life in the urgency of now. Eternity is in this moment. There is majesty in being in the world. We long for a vital center to our lives that both grounds us and inspires us, a vision of grander authenticity to our lives and not just smaller truths. All of us long for an evocative whole story and higher vision that lifts our hearts, pushes us to higher meanings, and ennobles our lives. Some may find that integrated story for the future is already here and now. The here is in the balanced secular life; the now is in the heart and mind, in reason and compassion, in accepting the exhilarating challenge of moving again toward a responsible search for truth and meaning. The now is also in committing to our highest meanings for a better life for all. As Humanists we know, as all wise people throughout the ages have known, that one needs meaning beyond oneself and one's own immediate happiness to achieve true fulfillment.

10

An Idea That Counts

Here is what I want. I simply wish to live in a just society, one that acts decently towards people and the planet. I want to work towards not just our well-being, but our flourishing in the small time we have here. That is enough. How we accomplish that, though, is immensely complex.

Although we have many tools in our ethical toolbox, I want to focus on just one powerful idea that is the first of our moral principles. I'll explain that in a moment. This idea is the one all Humanist authors and philosophers have pointed to. It is at once the most powerful and most demanding moral principle if we take it seriously. We have many ethical guideposts, but this one surely grounds many of the rest.

I fear we take it too much for granted, and do not understand well enough its origin, power and meaning in our own lives. More to the point, ideas matter and have real consequences. This is one of the very best. We would do well not to repeat it as yet another liberal mantra without serious consideration.

The principle I speak of is the one in the Humanist Manifesto III that says, "To affirm the inherent worth and dignity of each individual." Sometimes this is phrased as, "Affirming equal worth and dignity." What, exactly, does this mean? Does it mean that each of us is actually equal, in some radical egalitarian notion? Of course not. Common sense tells us that we are indeed sometimes vastly different in ability, behavior, morality, and usefulness to each other, indeed even in value to each other. If by worth we mean our relative worth to each other, the real truth is that we do judge each other by our own standards. In fact, we do regard each other differently. If one is totally relativistic, one could claim all judgments are relative and arbitrary. I do not make such a claim.

What did Thomas Jefferson mean in the Declaration of Independence when he said all men are created equal?

We are only deluding ourselves if we think of the inherent worth and dignity of each of us as something that is inherent in the world, is an objective truth, or is demonstrably true. This human worth and dignity is inherent, however, in the sense that we feel it our duty to confer worth and dignity as a right or privilege on every individual. The origin of this Humanist principle has its roots in the Enlightenment, when certain rights were attributed to people regardless of who they were.

The philosopher Immanuel Kant startled the world of his day with a different twist, showing that we should treat people as an end in themselves rather than a means. This was a revolutionary concept in its day. This means, in effect, that how useful or valuable a person is to us is not an appropriate measure for determining how we behave towards that person. Each person counts, no matter what their behavior or their utility to society or ourselves. We all have moral equivalence. He is saying that each of us has some inherent worth regardless of who he or she is and that each of us should enjoy some measure of dignity. No matter what.

The key idea that I would like to get across is that when we talk of each person's inherent worth and dignity, that statement should be interpreted as prescriptive, not descriptive. It's something we do, not something that is. Worth and dignity are things we are enjoined to give, not because they are in some sense "true," but because a rational morality depends on it. Doing this is something we find pragmatically useful. We use this idea because it works in the real court of human affairs. This is not a trivial difference of perspective.

The idea of equal worth and dignity asks us to "see" the other person as having worth despite any difference we may see in race, gender, nationality, sexual orientation, religion, age, ideology, morality, behavior or, indeed, anything. This does not ask us to diminish the importance of the very real differences between us. It does ask us to acknowledge our common humanity, joys, hopes, desires, fears and complex inner life. It is a realization that, despite our differences, we have a common core of human experience. Ignoring this fact leads to a world less capable of human moral worth. The truth of this statement is written through history in the rivers of blood when people did not affirm each individual's dignity and worth. This key idea is prescriptivism writ large.

There are four spheres where the concept of equal worth and dignity takes place: the personal, the interpersonal, the societal, and the planetary. Each carries a different perspective.

The personal. I suspect that at some point in each of our lives we have seriously questioned our own worth. One study in the United States found that seventy percent of all neuroses are bound up in shame of some sort. The 1971 Humanist of the Year, Albert Ellis, borrowed from ancient Greek and Roman stoic thinkers on the subject to develop Rational Emotive Behavioral Therapy (REBT). This is based on the simple principle that no one gives us self-esteem; we give it to ourselves. Our attitudes are products not of how the world is, but how we view it. Self-worth and self-esteem are a matter of choice and no one can give them or take them from us unless we allow it. It means we don't have to think alike or act alike to accept the humanity of others and ourselves. Ellis's idea of "unconditional self-acceptance" is a radical idea that works. In the work I do with addictions, I have seen its impact in patients' darkest hours. A crack-addicted prostitute, suicidal and shorn of all dignity and hope, grabbed onto the concept of unconditional self-acceptance and inherent worth and dignity as a life preserver. In a short time, she recovered successfully. Such is the power of an idea.

Liberalism, especially in the form called pluralism as coined by Isaiah Berlin, sees human diversity as a rational outcome. It tells us we don't need, nor should we expect, to find one rational way to live our lives. There are many ways to live the good life. As we saw earlier, Abraham Maslow saw self-acceptance as only the first step to a full life; persons extend their sphere of acceptance and identification outward as they mature. However, he believed one could not effectively deal with the other wider spheres of influence we will be talking about until wholly accepting oneself and believing in one's inherent worth.

The interpersonal. All the interpersonal self-help books out there might be boiled down to simply seeing the other person as human. Wasn't Dale Carnegie's self-improvement message nothing but acknowledging the other person's interests? We also see it in feminism, defined as the radical idea that women are people. This is why Gloria Steinem said she was a humanist before she became a feminist. It is so hard for us to get past seeing other people's differences that we can hardly see one another's humanity. Some might say this is just the Golden Rule, as expressed in many cultures. This concept, though, goes beyond the Golden Rule; it sees the other person as uniquely important.

Evolutionary psychology tells us we have instinctual prejudices against people different from us. Our task, I suggest, is to educate and work against our inherent tribalism. This is what makes us want people to look like us, act like us, and think like us. One of the tasks of a civilizing culture is to help us get past the differences and identify with the other. We know that, in fact, some cultures relish their tribalism and prejudice. Let's face it: it feels good to root for our tribe, whatever that is.

Encountering differences challenges us to get past even those aspects in others that we may judge as distasteful, wrong, or ugly and to see their inherent worth and dignity. Now, this is not just an idea, it is a practice. We don't have to fall into a superficial pluralism. By that I mean going to the extreme and saying behaviors, ideas and cultures are not sometimes important or should not be judged. There indeed are harmful and even evil ideas and cultures. This way of behaving asks that we not allow those negative aspects to interfere with our perception of the person's integral personhood. This is not easy work for any of us, for we are always at odds with our instincts that lead us towards prejudice. Talk is cheap, though. If we are not to be hypocrites, we have to walk the walk as well as talk the talk.

We can use imagery tools to help us. Martin Buber, the famous Jewish theologian and existentialist philosopher, used the linguistic tool of seeing each person not as a "you" (*Sie* in German) but as a "thou" (*du* in German) or a sacred, God-filled presence. Some Christians try to see God's love in each person. The stoic Roman emperor Marcus Aurelius said, "When men are inhuman, take care not to feel toward them as they do other humans." The Humanistic Albert Schweitzer spoke of a "reverence for life." Also, to overcome our implicit prejudice, we must continually endeavor to really listen to others and try to gain as much empathy as possible.

Regardless what tool we choose to use, it seems imperative to me that each of us find appropriate imagery to summon up so we can view each person as unique and worthy. At the same time, we must somehow separate all other factors, including both their behavior and their beliefs. Self-confessional time: seeing the humanity in people with extreme right wing opinions has been really tough for me. Still, I have found that if I try to see their humanity, something transformative happens to me. I feel better. I act better.

Societal. The third sphere of concern has to do with society. All our wars have a point where one group stops seeing the enemy as fully human. We use dehumanizing words like "Jap," "queer," "infidel," "gook," "savage," "raghead," or "red," which relieves us of moral duties to such non-human opponents. The psychologist Eric Ericson calls the process "de-speciation." The chief Sephardic rabbi in Israel once said one could not trust the Palestinians because they were "snakes."

Once we see another group of people as "the other," we can all the more easily see them as subhuman, not at all like ourselves, and set in motion our long human history of tribal, state and religious wars. This dehumanization ends in the ovens at Auschwitz, it ends in the killing fields of Cambodia, it ends in torture in the Abu Ghraib prison, and in the savagery we have become so used to seeing in the Middle East.

Those who die in any holocaust die because of an idea. The idea is that they are not like us and therefore not fully human so it is all right to kill them. In a movie about the trials at Nuremberg, one of the characters sought to answer the question of "What is evil?" His answer was, "When someone shows no sign of empathy."

But killing is done in a number of ways. For the underclass in America it is the slow death we perpetrate when we kill the spirit. When, in some states, we spend as much as four times for students in rich suburbs as we spend on students in inner cities and in rural areas, what we do is to kill hope and opportunity. We kill the spirit. One legislator in Illinois dismissed spending money to equalize educational opportunity in downstate districts as a losing proposition. His rationale: "They're just coal miners down there."

All of our civil rights, equal protection, equal justice, democracy, and equal opportunity are based on the principle of equal worth and dignity. When the Declaration of Independence said, "All men are created equal" and the French Revolution called for "Liberty, Equality and Fraternity," the voices of the Enlightenment had reached political fruition in a bold new experiment that now has shown its humanizing power.

But don't think the principle of inherent worth is universal. In fact most societies are tribal, and non-empathetic beyond the immediate family and tribe. Many Eastern scholars point out that the idea of universal empathy is a foreign concept in much of the East. Even though this is an idea that indeed works for all, it must not be assumed that it is a concept that is either natural or globally accepted.

The planetary. The empathy we show to other human beings should be shown to the biosphere as well. Seeing the glories of nature and its inherent worth is a skill, just like learning empathy towards humans. E. O. Wilson, the famous biologist and Humanist of the Year in 1999, points out that human beings have an instinctual biological drive towards what he calls biophilia. He argues that biodiversity should be nurtured, not just for its economic usefulness, but equally to nurture our own inherent need to feel complete and at one with nature. Seeing nature as having inherent worth rather than a means to some end is an important transformation. It is seeing ourselves imbedded in and not apart from nature.

In war we see two types of soldiers. One type uses war as an excuse to let their basest emotions play out and not see the underlying humanity in others. US Army Lt. William Calley, who participated in the My Lai massacre in

Vietnam, is just such an example. Conversely, there were those who never reduced others and themselves to barbarism. There were those who kept their sense of humanity.

Our paths through life are all different, but each of us learned these principles somewhere because they are universal to the human condition. Along the way we find ideas that serve us better than others. If we hold to the idea that we want a better world, we are challenged to embrace the inherent worth of every individual and of our planet. This is not because it is "true," but because it works. Experience shows clearly where not doing so leads. When we see ourselves as less than fully human, it results in shame. When we can't see the core humanity in others, we see only their differences and flaws. When our inherent tribalism darkens our view of other groups, then prejudice, oppression and war surely follow. And when our connections with nature's inherent worth are lost, our planet is lost.

Humanists are committed to that very Western Enlightenment idea that every child and every human being's heart is our heart; their dreams are our dreams; and their fears and their loves are ours as well. Set alone on this small planet, we have only ourselves to set things right. We must all breathe the common air of freedom, justice, worth and dignity to be fully and most fruitfully and joyously alive. As the American poet Langston Hughes put it:

I dream a world where man
No other man will scorn
Where love will bless the earth
And peace its paths adorn

11

Religion II

Let us now expand on the issue of religion. You may have been a practicing member of a religious community; maybe you are still in one, or maybe you never were in one. Regardless, we are all affected by religion as part of our own history and culture. We can dismiss God beliefs and still try to understand the religious impulses and see what we can learn from them, especially about ourselves. As they say, take the best and leave the rest.

The varieties of religion are endless. There is no such thing as Christianity; there are Christianities—in fact, thousands of Christian sects and denominations. *The World Christian Encyclopedia* of 2001 counted 33,830. No one can argue that the Amish, Mormons, Catholics, Evangelicals, Jehovah's Witnesses, and members of the more liberal United Church of Christ are remotely similar. Likewise, there is no such thing as Buddhism; there are many Buddhisms. One could even argue that a distinctive American Buddhism has evolved into a completely separate religion today. Thus, we have to be careful of overgeneralizing about what religions entail to ensure that we realize the incredible diversity present today.

The first thing that dominates any serious study of religion is the instinctual impulse to build and participate in community. I may have a lot of criticisms of evangelical religion, but at least it offers a supportive home in a mobile, alienated, world. I'm convinced that a lot of people would be a lot crazier if they didn't have a nurturing community to support them. Many scholars studying the sociology of religion say that community is the number one factor that makes people stay in religion. Many people participate who don't even believe any of the dogma, but like the community and a bit of the pageantry. We all know of people who just laugh off their religion's nonsense aspects, but still participate in their church's community, who are sometimes referred to as "Jack Catholics" or "Jack Mormons".

Religion may be the dead hand of superstition and may be losing its ideological binding force, but the need for community is universal. We long for belonging. We are social creatures, happiest when we enjoy the support of a nurturing community. Some Humanists may be more loners. If that is what they want, it's fine, but I think all of us want to connect with others in some way. It is only through others that we know ourselves. Additionally, many studies have concluded that being in a community makes us happier and emotionally healthier and helps us live longer. So if we give up traditional religion, what options do we have if we enjoy community, remembering none of us absolutely need community? Today most leaving religious communities generally don't join an alternate community.

A number of specifically secular groups exist, including American Humanist Association chapters, Freedom From Religion Foundation chapters, American Atheist chapters, American Ethical Union societies, Unitarian Universalist congregations, Society for Humanistic Judaism, Sunday Assemblies, and numerous others. Most of these are small and do not have the elaborate support systems that many churches do. Many are just learning how to "do" community, as a number of skill sets are required to build an intentional community. In addition, think of all the communities we are involved in such as youth sports, political parties, social action groups, and even online communities. Still, we can learn much from the religious congregations that are good at creating and sustaining intentional communities.

It is great if you are lucky enough to have a community of friends that support you. In Europe, the churches are all but empty. The joke there is that people go to church only three times anymore. Two of those times they are carried in: hatching; matching; and dispatching. The large cathedrals and churches are mostly museums. Many of the rest are, as one European friend said, "usually the best restaurants and nightclubs in town." Europeans may not need church because they have been informed by a centuries old Humanist culture. Generally their Humanist community is the community at large. The European Western Enlightenment tradition of Humanism is deeply imbedded in their culture, unlike the United States where religion has been and is still a dominant force in our culture.

Fundamentally, we tribal apes thrive in small communities of 150 members or less. Dunbar's number, as this is known, is the approximate maximum of members in a community. Larger groups start to fracture and split because it's hard to maintain social relationships with more than around 150 people. The traditional Hutterite religious communities purposely divide when they get to around that number.

In the case of Humanists, if you find that you need community, try to find one that supports you in your journey of life. Remember, no one is as smart as all of us. Communities can stifle growth or stimulate it, so choose wisely.

Another religious impulse is the need for ceremony and ritual. Few of us want to have a birthday without a celebration of some kind. Catholics have been perfecting the high mass for centuries and it is an incredible show. Their stagecraft engages all the senses including high vaulted ceilings reaching toward the heavens, the heavy scent of incense, the ethereal mesmerizing Gregorian chanting, the lavish costumes, and the carefully choreographed liturgy, which reaches a dramatic peak like an opera with the consecration.

Modern religion has commodified techniques that are successful in bringing peace and comfort rather than being merely doctrinaire. While *Christianity Today* reports that America has 250,000 Protestant churches, 200,000 are either stagnant (with no growth) or declining. That is 80 percent of the Protestant churches in America. Four thousand churches close their doors every single year. At the same time the Leadership Network & Hartford Institute reported that modern megachurches with over two thousand members showed a median growth rate of 26 percent over five years—or more than 5 percent a year on average. Many of these are modeled after the Willow Creek church in Barrington, Illinois. Typically they are giant windowless boxes with low lighting until lights on the stage explode in your eyes like a rock show, and indeed a Christian rock band blasts forth. Ceremony in a megachurch can be more like a rock concert than a traditional worship service.

This is a whole different experience than in the Catholic Church or smaller, more intimate churches. It is a passively watched show, similar to watching TV. Megachurches get growth beyond Dunbar's number by plugging people into small cluster groups with similar needs. This way they achieve intimacy and group solidarity. If you are a divorced single woman with children and an alcohol problem, your nearest megachurch probably has a group or even several for you. This allows one to find intimacy with someone even in the midst of a congregation of thousands.

Islam likewise uses captivating ceremony, starting with the minaret call to prayer and the Koran's poetic Arabic language that often brings men and women to tears. Consider the rhythmic Buddhist chanting and prayer wheels. All religions and, in fact, all cultures employ ceremony and ritual, especially at important times of passage such as birth, coming of age, marriage, and death. Most secular people have a need to commemorate and remember these important times as well.

Humanist celebrants or officiants provide services to commemorate times of passage for the secular, focusing on creating a meaningful experience that's specific to the person. If you desire to commemorate and celebrate a life passage, know that a unique, personal ceremony can be developed that speaks to your own life. A Humanist ceremony need be neither emotionally sterile nor emotionally manipulative to memorialize what is truest to us.

In Norway today, more than ten thousand teenagers around the age of 15 go through a Humanist coming of age ceremony every year, or around 17 percent of the target market. In Scotland, more secular marriages take place than religious ones. In Ireland, Humanist celebrants are booked up more than a year in advance.

Death has a special meaning for all of us. Humanists generally celebrate a person's life in a memorial service and try to bring some measure of closure to the deceased's family and friends. We mourn the death and celebrate the life of loved ones because our heart longs to be heard. Most of us want to give voice to our grief and to seek the comfort of one another.

Most feel we need to commemorate these life passages in a way that doesn't compromise our integrity, but provides an evocative experience that is true to the person. It can be and is being done all the time.

Religion is in many ways defined by what is called the religious experience. William James's book, *The Varieties of Religious Experience*, is still a great classic on the subject. He noted that mystical religious experiences are ineffable, the experience all but impossible to communicate, but revelatory and full of meaning, despite the fact that they are inarticulate experiences.

The experience may be a "spiritual awakening" that leads to a transformation because one feels enlightened with some new knowledge. It can be an epiphany leading to long term commitments, changes, and priorities. There can be a feeling of oneness with the universe and others, of a connectedness, peacefulness, and overpowering sense of awe.

Religious experiences can be brought on by praying, music, dance, such as the Sufi whirling dervishes, psycho-tropic drugs, temporal lobe epilepsy, meditation, schizo-phrenia, brain probing and even electromagnetic pulses generated in what is called the "God helmet."

There is no doubt these experiences of altered states of consciousness can have a profound effect on those having them. They can have a unifying feeling. Their revelatory aspects can change lives. Paul's experience on the road to Damascus, if true, launched a new form of religion: many scholars believe most of Christianity is really Pauline in nature.

For Humanists, we can and do have these numinous experiences as well, but where our approach is different is in how we interpret these experiences. I once almost died from a burst appendix, experienced tunnel vision, and saw a bright light. I interpreted this as, "Oh my, I have a 106-degree Fahrenheit fever and my brain is frying and I may be dying." I almost did die. That is the ratio-nal, scientific, medical interpretation. I was experiencing my brain starting to "spark" and "short circuit" as it was shutting down.

Abraham Maslow postulated that emotionally healthy individuals can have "peak experiences" in which one loses one's ego in a rapturous heightened consciousness. Mihály Csíkszentmihályi calls these experiences "flow." Most people have had them. In my own case, as a young boy I found an old discarded record and heard Enrico Caruso sing "Celeste Aida." I knew nothing of opera or classical music, but knew this was magic. It was transformative for me, leading me to love opera and classical music. I experienced the same result listening to Eric Clapton playing "Layla." I once found myself ethereally transported while looking at a sunrise at Dead Horse Point in Utah. Haven't you had these experiences that gave you chills and goosebumps?

We can enjoy these experiences, but as I noted, we can interpret them many ways. Some would see God's handiwork in a sunrise, but we Humanists can experience totally naturalistic awe and wonder. It's a good thing we have these moments. They really are the spice of life; we can remember them for years and they can be a motive force for good in our lives. Awe and wonder are not only experienced by the religious. We, too, have experiences that engender a feeling of connectedness, wholeness, and unity.

There are dangers, though, in letting ecstasy lead us astray. Life presents us with small windows into other lives, and I once had a personal experience that was awakening to me. It was on a blistering hot day some years ago while on vacation. I was pulled into a volleyball tournament in Florida and was teamed with two elderly, but very athletic, in-shape men. We sat down after having finished a couple of games, exhausted, sweltering and dying of thirst. Sitting in the shade of a great live oak tree we downed glass after glass of water and I heard bits and pieces of German conversation about their experiences as soldiers. Speaking a little German, I asked them if they had been soldiers in the German Army in World War II. They both acknowledged this and said they had even been boyhood friends.

I knew this was one of those rare moments where I was being given an opportunity to peer into another's life, to see important first-hand history through their eyes. I also knew I needed to put on my best neutral, non-judgmental

face, and use this as a learning experience. I said it must
have been rough in the war and they said it was indeed
horrible and recounted how they had luckily escaped
death despite having been captured by the Soviets, who
usually executed German prisoners. Returning home they
found 90 percent of their village had been destroyed and
their families were all dead. Like many older people it
was obvious they could vividly remember every detail
of their youth better than last week.

I asked if he had been at the huge Nuremburg Nazi
rallies. With eyes wide open, still looking up, he said,
"We were at all the rallies and it was fantastic to be part
of it, the long rows of soldiers at attention, the music, the
speeches."

I then hesitatingly asked the big question, "Had you
ever seen Hitler?"

"Oh yes," one replied, "many times, in fact, as we were
in the Hitler Youth corps."

"What was he like?" I asked, expecting some cautiously
polite answer.

Picture two old men, sitting cross-legged, hunched on
the ground, sweating, and exhausted; the one speaking sat
up slowly, back straightening, and with a swelling chest
looked skyward and said, "He was wonderful." This was
a man in a religious thrall. He was fourteen years of age
back in Germany, emotionally ecstatic.

"What was so great about him?" I asked.

"He gave us everything," he said. "Growing up, we
had nothing. We were lucky to have a potato every other
day. My mother made my pants out of an old burlap seed
sack. After Hitler we had beautiful uniforms and food. He
gave us everything."

I didn't want to break their trust, but asked, how they could think so highly of Hitler and the Nazi movement when they, more than most, knew the real costs of war, the real horrors of where the Nazi ideology had led. This broke his reverie for a moment and his back slumped. He reaffirmed that it had indeed been horrible and that the experience had deeply pained his whole life. But then again with a rising, stiffening back he looked skyward and said, "But it was a wonderful time, too." I recalled Hannah Arendt's description at the Nuremburg trials of the "banality of evil" seeing how normal they appeared.

This experience made me deeply aware that the ecstatic religious experience of awe, deep emotional commitment, and a totalizing philosophy can be secular as well as religious and can have equally disastrous results. After this I joined my wife, who said I appeared ashen and inquired what was wrong. I replied that I had just met two unrepentant Nazis who otherwise had seemed quite normal.

Haven't you had oceanic ecstatic experiences? Maybe at a rock concert, listening to music at home, falling in love, observing nature, during sex, singing in a chorus, at your marriage, and even while on drugs? Sure you have, almost certainly. There are incredibly powerful experiences that are transformative, dripping with life-long memories. They make life worth living. And yet: they can lead us to believe lies, to commit ourselves to horrible evils, to "group think," and the loss of reason.

The dilemma we all face is to avoid becoming head-only rationalists devoid of passion, and on the other hand to avoid ecstatic experiences that take us down dark paths. We still somehow need evocative experiences that nurture our highest and noblest aspirations.

Religion is such a powerful force in people's lives that we would be foolish not to mine it for the gems we seculars can use. Take for example the concepts of salvation, redemption, and forgiveness in Christianity. These are great secular concepts as well if we get rid of their theological aspects. We all could use a little more forgiveness and, yes, we can change for the better when we believe our lives are redeemable. Some Christians, especially Catholics, remind us to love our neighbor as ourselves and to help the poor and disadvantaged. These are great secular sentiments as well.

Christianity grew rapidly among slaves in ancient Rome as it offered hope to those with none. Christianity offered the hope of a heavenly reward, but we Humanists have to remind ourselves that hope in the here and now is needed to survive difficult times.

Buddhism is generally nontheistic, especially Theravada Buddhism, although Mahayana Buddhism is more supernatural. Buddhism reminds us, with the Eight-fold Path, to practice right view, intention, speech, action, livelihood, effort, mindfulness and concentration. These are very similar to Aristotle's virtues. Buddhism makes us aware that impermanence is a fact of life and that much of our suffering comes from unhealthy desire. These are great universal lessons about life. The Buddhist tradition has developed sophisticated meditation techniques; their emphasis on mindfulness, that is, gathering one's total focused attention, living in the present moment, and being able to ignore distractions can be an extremely helpful technique. All of us can use more attentiveness, more deep awareness in our lives.

Buddhism is well known for its efforts in many areas to encourage peace and nonviolence. It is a great practice for Humanists to follow as well. Nevertheless, as in all religions, the moral philosophy may not match the moral practice. The violence in Buddhist monasteries by masters over their students can be appalling; the war on Muslims by Buddhists in Myanmar (Burma) recently reached genocidal proportions.

Taoism is a great nontheistic tradition that teaches moral virtue and living in harmony with nature. Confucianism is a secular moral philosophy and provides general prescriptions for life.

Even Islam can show us something of value. While Islam is the most religiously intolerant religion, it is the most racially tolerant.

I don't mean to be an apologist for religion here, but we must always be open to ideas that work for the greater good, regardless of their origin. The Humanist Press publishes *A Jefferson Bible for the Twenty-first Century*, which lists "best of" and "worst of" scriptural citations for Islam, Buddhism, Hinduism, Judaism, Mormonism, and Christianity. None of these religions would have been successful if they weren't doing some things right. We are fools if don't learn what we can from them.

We may tend to see people and religions in neat little categories, but we all know this isn't true. Entering the twenty-first century, the sociologist of religion Wade Clark Roof sees an America where "Boundaries separating one faith tradition from another that once seemed fixed are now often blurred; religious identifications are malleable and multifaceted, often overlapping several traditions." People have learned to embrace and syncretize many different religious beliefs and practices. We now see yoga classes in churches and meditation practices even in evangelical churches. Traditional religion and in particular institutional religion continues to lose influence while at the same time individualistic religion dominates.

Today, ultimate authority for religious meaning comes not from institutional authority, science, or reason, but from inner existential and experiential voices. Its truths are less and less objective and almost exclusively subjective. The locus of meaning has been driven into the well of direct experience and the authority of the individual. In many cases the Emersonian transcendental urge is fulfilled with an image of a God of immanence within oneself. This has to do more with feelings and awareness that are authentic only to the individual. Religion, always a meaning-making story, is only authentic today if it is our story. The "sacred" is what is sacred only to us. For religion to be true and meaningful, it must emanate from our own experiences.

We now have a generalized, syncretized, enigmatic "fuzzy theism" that is intuitional, variable, and individualized, and yet has similar attributes in some regards. It embraces a "God" who adapts to the situation, sometimes morphing into merely "an energy in the universe," sometimes morphing into the creator God, sometimes framed in terms of the indeterminacy of quantum mechanics, and mostly having the uplifting characteristics of American optimism and reassurance.

This modern religiousness is increasingly based not on an intellectually reflective theology so much as a purely experiential one. The mantra today is, "I'm spiritual, not religious," keeping it just vague enough not to offend others, while providing a pretense of moral piousness. The word "spirituality" sells well because it is a Rorschach test for everyone's view of what is emotionally important to them. But the term may neither inform nor communicate. Most important, it skews religion toward a God of everlasting inwardness. Much of religion today has shifted from dogmatic top-down authoritarianism to the "Church of the Greater Solipsism."

Many Humanists claim a spirituality of their own. For Humanists who use the term spirituality, it expresses the deepest emotional commitments that transcend our day-to-day living, but is totally naturalistic. It is a summary of all that animates their lives. The author Parker Palmer's definition is "Spirituality is the eternal human longing to be connected to something larger than one's ego." It is the sum of all our connectedness, meanings, and values. For many Humanists, "spirituality" expresses in one simple word their emotional commitments, born from reason, about their deepest life commitments, those that unify the self. These orientations are a good thing, I think. For others, however, the word "spirituality" is too loaded with theological implications that can't be unwound.

I have no problem with a Humanist spirituality that expresses something many Humanists find useful, as long as it maintains a here-and-now non-supernatural orientation and is not a tool for emotional manipulation. Carl Sagan wrote, "Science is not only compatible with spirituality; it is a profound source of spirituality. When we recognize our place in an immensity of light-years and in the passage of ages, when we grasp the intricacy, beauty, and subtlety of life, then that soaring feeling, that sense of elation and humility combined, is surely spiritual." He elaborated on this idea: "Such are our emotions in the presence of great art or music or literature or of acts of exemplary selfless courage by those such as Mohandas Gandhi or Martin Luther King, Jr. The notion that science and spirituality are mutually exclusive does a disservice to both."

Still, we have to be careful. Language can be a manipulative tool that lets us pretend we are all talking about the same things, when in fact we have irresolvable differences. Spirituality may use such a broad-based metaphor that it can prevent us from really saying what we mean; using specific language would be far better. We may know what we mean, but others may not. For example, rather than "spiritual" it might be better to be specific and say, "My feelings of connected wholeness and purpose," or "That which emotionally uplifts me," or "Commitments that are transcendent to me," or "God talks to me and fills me with love," etc.; whatever is the true meaning we want to get across. We need not pretend we are all talking about the same thing when we use the word "spiritual" with others. Generally we are not, and we can have radical differences.

There is an ethics of words. It requires us to be honest with our language and to bear responsibility that our communication is not misunderstood. It requires that we know when and where to use metaphor and when to use specific descriptive language. It means we must responsibly ensure that the listener understands what we really mean. Say what you mean, and mean what you say. Sometimes it may be better not to use the word "spirituality," not because it doesn't mean anything, but because it means too much. Determine your audience and the specifics of what you really mean and communicate it to the listener without obfuscation. Still, there is something of great value in embracing a Humanist life stance that speaks to all that we are in ineffable and evocative ways.

Within theological schools is a school of thought called "process theology" that originally was developed out of ideas of the philosopher Alfred North Whitehead, later given real voice by Charles Hartshorne, John B. Cobb, Jr., and David Ray Griffin. Hartshorne postulated a "panentheism" (all is in God) that must be differentiated from "pantheism" (all is God) and tries to blend religion with science in a semi-naturalistic way. Process theology sees God as immanent in the world and in us rather than transcendent.

This muddle of words and enigmatic distinctions is given great credence in liberal theological schools. The billionaire financier John Templeton became enamored with process theology and set up an annual "Templeton Prize for Progress Toward Research or Discoveries about Spiritual Realities," whose annual award is larger than the Nobel Prize. The fight for the prize money in theological schools has managed to legitimize the notion that supernatural theological ideas have a scientific basis. But note the title of the prize, which presupposes the premise that there actually are spiritual realities. Follow the money, really, really big money: $2.9 billion in the fund in 2015. This mouthwatering financial carrot has influenced all theological schools and theology in general.

Process theology is only one part of a whole theological shift from the identifiable personal God of Abrahamic religions to the variety of vague notions of God we have today. We now have the process theological God who is part of all that is, but not quite pantheistic.

We have other variances on the god idea. We have the "God of the gaps" because some are uncomfortable with their own ignorance. The fact is that science keeps shrinking the unknown and the world becomes increasingly knowable. It is telling that this unexplained mystery is always spoken of in hushed tones. The so-called "God of the gaps" keeps shrinking and is increasingly untenable intellectually. As Einstein said, "The most incomprehensible thing about the universe is that it is comprehensible." And as the English writer Eden Phillpotts said, "The universe is full of magical things, patiently waiting for our wits to grow sharper."

Religion for most is but a thin cloth over what is really a pragmatic secular life. The critic Harold Bloom, in *The American Religion*, sees American religion as unique, embodying a Gnosticism centered on personal experience. "The God of American religion is an experiential God, so radically within our own being as to become a virtual identity with what is most authentic (oldest and best) in the self." As the historian R. Laurence Moore pointed out in *Selling God*, religion in America is a commodity of the self. Traditional notions of God are being redefined by all. The center does not hold in any religious tradition; we hear the words "preference" and "opinion" replacing traditionalism and dogmatism in this world of postmodern self-referential relativism.

While the trend toward the religion of self-referentiality continues and mainline religions are dying, fundamentalism grows more strident. The religious scholar Martin Marty studied worldwide fundamentalism for years. He documented in his five-volume *Fundamentalism Project* that fundamentalism does not occur out of strength, but as a last resort when a religion is in its death throes. This doubling down and intransigence is a fear response out of weakness. We can see it in the Middle East where Muslims feel under attack by Western modernism. In the United States, we see the total radicalization and polarization of Christianity. The growth of an intransigent religious right that refuses to deal with facts, compromise, or self-reflection is particularly problematic for Humanists, particularly where these fundamentalists consider Humanists tools of Satan. The result has been great discrimination against Humanists.

So how should Humanism respond to religion? More important, how should you respond? There is no easy or right answer. Humanists respond in a range from a live-and-let-live, respectful tolerance to an in-your-face antitheism. There are good arguments for needing both strategies simultaneously. Religion unquestionably helps some people. The big question each of us may ask is, "Does the balance of good outweigh the bad regarding religion?"

Personally, I tend to gravitate toward an antitheist pole, seeing traditional religion and even God belief as being harmful on balance to individuals and society. Even still, I must admit that I may be wrong in this assessment and maybe a live-and-let-live, respectful tolerance might be better for everyone. I do feel pretty strongly that hubris and intolerance are dangerous to us and we need the whole range of secular voices about religion. As the atheist writer Greta Christina said, we need both the "firebrands and the diplomats." In real everyday life, each situation demands a pragmatic, situational assessment. Any rigidness or ideology is dangerous. Tolerance still should guide our behavior toward others' beliefs, but be balanced with critical thinking. When people's beliefs turn into actions, that is a different story.

There is also the religious impulse as a grounding experience to integrate our whole life. We will talk more about this in later chapters, but, for now, keep in mind that religion tries to put together an integrated story of life. The stories vary tremendously, but like the tale of the hunter-gatherers around the fire long ago, they give people answers for living. More important, both religion and Humanism give meaningful purpose to our lives. Humanism can give us an evocative integrative experience just as religion does, but without all the supernatural stuff, and as true to reality as we can make it.

12

Civilization

"Civilization is to groups what intelligence is to individuals. It is a means of combining the intelligence of many to achieve ongoing group adaptation. Civilization, like intelligence, may serve well, serve adequately, or fail to serve its adaptive function. When civilization fails to serve, it must disintegrate unless it is acted upon by unifying internal or external forces."
— Octavia E. Butler, *Parable of the Sower*

As pointed out earlier, some words are not given to simple definitions and any single definition is bound to be incomplete and to distort. So it is with the concept of civilization, the best repository of our cultural memory. Many identify it with the growth of cities and their accompanying cultures. I like to think of Humanism as representing the best fruits of the civilization that emerged in several places around the globe around 3300 BCE, advancing rapidly around 500 BCE, and evolving until the present day. Evolving like science, civilization emerges from the experience of what actually works in society. Writing, laws, democracy, division of labor, technology, art and architecture, political structures, and currency were parts of what were found to work.

A more important lesson is how we treat one another. As Jane Addams, a social reformer and a member of the Chicago Humanist Society, once said, "Civilization is a method of living, an attitude of equal respect for all men." Note that this echoes the views in Chapter 10. Sigmund Freud said, "The first human who hurled an insult instead of a stone was the founder of civilization."

Humanism embraces the totality of everything history has taught us about how best to live. It requires of us a broad range of knowledge and sympathies.

I've been surprised at how many people I've met in the secular movement who dismiss literary fiction, saying they're interested only in reading nonfiction and, more specifically, important scientific books. Some seculars have edged nearer and even crossed over to scientism—the overvaluing of the ability of science to inform and guide us in how to live our secular lives. The philosopher Daniel Dennett warned us in his book *Darwin's Dangerous Idea*, "There is no such thing as philosophy-free science; there is only science whose philosophical baggage is taken on board without examination." Dismissing the humanities is problematic for Humanists, who have been some of the few willing to stand up for reason and science in our neoromantic, postmodern, counter-enlightenment, religion-dominated times. We don't want to appear to disparage science. Still, history repeatedly calls for a balanced, interdisciplinary approach to Humanism. The humanities have much to inform us and we disregard them at great loss, as modern Humanism represents the best of both the Enlightenment and the Romantic traditions.

Fourteenth-century Renaissance Humanism— inspired by the classical literature of Greece and Rome—emerged out of the Dark Ages with a focus on human welfare and potential. The Italian scholar Petrarch heralded our potential for progress and a higher culture focused on humanity, not God. The Renaissance gave great importance to the artistic community. Benefactors like the Medici family helped advance our cultural civilization. Cosimo de' Medici built the library of San Marco to house the texts that informed the Renaissance Humanists. The English novelist John Fowles commented on its importance: "In essence the Renaissance was simply the green end of one of civilization's hardest winters."

Why are the humanities so important? What value do music, literature, philosophy, history, art, drama, architecture, and poetry have, other than to provide us with pleasure? This perennial question has been answered many times, but we still seem to forget that even today Shakespeare still tells us more about human character than most psychological science, that Greek sculpture reflects our highest visions of the human form, that Samuel Barber's *Adagio for Strings* musically make us aware of beauty's higher reaches, and gangster rap speaks to the angst of urban despair.

Charles Dickens' marginalized characters inhabit our minds long after reading about them. Elie Wiesel's book *Night* sears our heart with the consequences of bigotry. No one needs Enlightenment rationalism to understand the horror of slavery after seeing the movie *Twelve Years a*

Slave. The earlier story of the child imprisoned in *Omelas* makes the importance of human dignity a visceral awareness. None of these are examples of scientific learning. They are experiential, transformative lessons separate from "head-only" thinking. As the painter Georges Braque said, "Art upsets, science reassures."

Put another way, we can rationally "know" things, but by making things real and immediate, art makes us emotionally aware. Great art holds up a mirror to us, our lives, and our societies in ways no mere data can. As Albert Camus said, "If the world were clear there would be no need for art." Maybe it's true what George Bernard Shaw said: "Without art, the crudeness of reality would make the world unbearable." Yes, art entertains, but it also opens doors to knowing and to awareness we might not otherwise possess. It arouses us to action. Art can be transformative.

The philosopher George Santayana said, "To feel beauty is a better thing than to understand how we come to feel it. To have imagination and taste, to love the best, to be carried by the contemplation of nature to *a vivid faith in the ideal*, all this is more, a great deal more, than any science can hope to be." When Santayana refers to "A vivid faith in the ideal," he is taking about Humanism.

Other humanities need our attention as well, most importantly, philosophy. Massimo Pigliucci and others find the increasing dominance of a scientific approach a sad turn of affairs for atheism and Humanism and they have challenged the writings of some seculars. I agree. Philosophy, despite its problems, still offers conceptual and critical thinking tools to understand reality. Pigliucci distinguishes two kinds of knowledge. The first type he calls *scientia*, which consists of science, philosophy, logic, and math. The second includes literature, the arts, and other humanities.

Many times a purely scientific approach leads some to mere reductionism, whereas the humanities enlighten us about life's emergent complexities, from hearts that ache, hopes that soar, our longings for better life, and the moral life within.

As Pigliucci said about science, "There is important stuff before it: there are human emotions, expressed by literature, music and the visual arts; there is culture; there is history. The best understanding of the whole shebang that humanity can hope for will involve a continuous dialogue between all our various disciplines." Indeed, pulling together all our human resources is what civilization entails. This inspires a full, robust Humanism beyond mere atheism or mere scientism. Raising our consciousness and increasing our sensitivity may be just as important for obtaining the good life as knowing true facts about the world.

Kenneth Clark wrote in his seminal book, *Civilization*, "I believe order is better than chaos, creation better than destruction. I prefer gentleness to violence, forgiveness to vendetta. On the whole I think that knowledge is preferable to ignorance, and I am sure that human sympathy is more valuable than ideology. I believe that in spite of the recent triumphs of science, men haven't changed much in the last two thousand years; and in consequence we must try to learn from history."

Scholars who have studied why some societies thrive and others don't point toward what is called "cultural capital," which is another way of saying civilization. The members of successful societies cultivate mutual trust, human solidarity, and peace as well as all of civilization's material benefits.

Max Weber, one of the founders of the modern science of sociology, noted that the fate of our times is characterized by rationalization and intellectualization and, above all, by the "disenchantment of the world." He was concerned that with the loss of religion, people would lose an emotional connection with the world. "And then," in the words of Kenneth Clark, "exhaustion, the feeling of hopelessness which can overtake people even with a high degree of material prosperity" would take over.

Nietzsche before them asked, "If God is dead, what then?" The German philosopher Martin Heidegger offered this answer to the problem of nihilism: "If God as the suprasensory ground and goal of all reality is dead, if the suprasensory world of the ideas has suffered the loss of its obligatory and above it its vitalizing and upbuilding power, then nothing more remains to which man can cling and by which he can orient himself."

Nonsense. Our answer to this call for a vitalizing, upbuilding power of life is Humanism. We have empirical evidence of this in secular countries such as in Europe, Australia, and Japan that provide examples of how we can, indeed, be good without God.

Many coming out of religion, as I did, go through the angry "come-outer" stage. Most move on to a more reflective, encompassing Humanism, but some do not. In the early stages it seems helpful to vent, but then try to turn that energy to a more positive and productive activism. It is understandable that as a marginalized, oppressed segment of society, we Humanists will attract those whose frustrations may boil over. But it simply is not enough to know only what one is *against*. Rather, to move beyond anger, one must come to know what to be *for*.

Nevertheless, I have seen too many who found one great truth, that God doesn't exist, and stopped their search there. I have seen those who don't have a vital center to their lives and fall into a "nihilistic disenchantment." This is one of my primary concerns for our culture, indeed for all of civilization, as we become more secular. There is too much toxic individualism today and not enough civic engagement.

Civilization can both stultify and edify, so we have to look critically at what is the good life and a good society. What may look like a noble culture to some may be merely a system of power and control to others, so we must always remain skeptical and self-aware of where we are going wrong.

Civilization is fragile. I believe Humanism not only springs from the well of civilization, but at the same time is the only thing that can save it at this point in history. Anti-government ideology can descend to a cancerous form of civilization suicide. Kenneth Clark warned us, "It is lack of confidence, more than anything else, that kills a civilization. We can destroy ourselves by cynicism and disillusion, just as effectively as by bombs."

W. B. Yeats wrote these famous, prophetic lines as a warning:

Things fall apart; the centre cannot hold;
Mere anarchy is loosed upon the world,
The blood-dimmed tide is loosed, and everywhere
The ceremony of innocence is drowned;

The best of us lack all conviction, while the worst
Are full of passionate intensity.

Some have asked why I am such a devoted social activist. It's because I believe the forces of barbarism are, and
have always been, all around us. I also believe it is both
our duty and our joy to defend the highest forms of civilization. Today the tides of barbarism have risen higher
than they have been for a long time. Martin Luther King,
Jr. warned us, "A nation or civilization that continues to
produce soft-minded men purchases its own spiritual
death on the installment plan." Apathy and cynicism are
civilization's soft underbelly. The culture that inspires
constant renewal, love, imagination, and a devotion to
truth is best able to expand and protect civilization.

13

Pitfalls to Avoid in Humanism

Humanism has wonderful things to offer, but like any world view we need to be careful about some pitfalls. We are only human and can lose our way, as all humans do.

Humanism asks that we seek the best for ourselves and society. Some might erroneously read that to mean Humanism is only for a highly educated, highly sophisticated, elite and privileged minority. Some of the subjects in this book, which we've only touched on, can be challenging. Is there no room for everyone else, including the inexperienced, unrefined, or otherwise ordinary? Of course there is. Humanists span the entire spectrum of class, education, and economic wealth, even though it is true that the organized movement historically has been dominated more by intellectuals. I like to think that those in our movement who have been fortunate in life know it, and have been motivated to making the world better for all. We have the whole range of people in our movement, all of whom seem to "get it" regardless of background.

More important, billions are living full and rich secular lives without even being in the secular movement.

Looking for intellectual depth in Humanism's foundations is not simple. It might be threatening and confusing to some yet overly simplistic for others. Regardless, our essential message is actually pretty straightforward. As the early Humanist pioneer Ray Bragg said, "This world is all and enough." It gets difficult after that. Our task is to reach as wide an audience as possible.

Reason itself has been questioned by many, as it can be a tool to rationalize power and control. For example, one can provide very good rational reasons why one needs more information on people's lives including medical, criminal, tax, housing, educational and genetic data. Looking reductively at each specific piece of information, one can build fair arguments for why a government or employer needs to collect it. Only when we expand our view do we see the frightening prospect of others using that data to justify prejudices and to deploy knowledge as a weapon. Reason can "rationally justify" one side or another of many ethical dilemmas such as freedom vs. security, and merely become a rationalization for our prejudices. Many evolutionary psychologists think reason was developed not to find the truth, but to win arguments.

Some consider that bureaucracies are a natural outcome of narrow rationalistic processes. The idea is that they are built for many small, sound, rational reasons, but ultimately ignore the eventual irrational result: an inoperable, oppressive, clumsy, and inefficient system. Likewise, bureaucracies can be coldly calculating and quite inhuman. Another example of a narrowly conceived rationality is an assembly line, where looking only at its "rational economic efficiency" may ignore that efficiency's human toll.

Billions of people live on the edge of survival, education, and cultural support. They have no need for fancy talk and have no time to delve into the depths of philosophy. They need voices that reach them where they are and honor where they are in their own journeys. Just because some of us have been privileged to be able to explore Humanism at deeper levels does not mean everyone needs or wants to, or should do so. Maybe you have been fortunate enough to be of the right country, sex, class, and race to obtain all the tools needed for an advanced and advantaged Humanism. We must always then be aware of being in a privileged position. We can't just stay on the periphery of issues, but must actively work to alleviate the structural problems that keep everyone from enjoying a full, rich life.

We can use Abraham Maslow's hierarchy of needs to explain how many of us get opportunities to become fully actualized after all our other needs for basic survival, safety, and social thriving are met. Many others are just trying to survive, just trying to stay safe, just trying to overcome addictions or discrimination, just trying to get any education at all, just trying to find any community of love and support. We need to create a Humanistic narrative that every person, regardless of their situation, will find compelling.

The disenfranchised in our communities too often have no voice and become invisible. Women are still marginalized in subtle ways even though they have made great strides. African Americans, Latinos, Muslims, and Asian Americans become targets for easy discrimination and are silenced at every turn. Since the Stonewall riots, LGBT people have also reduced the stigma of their gender identity, but we know prejudice is still rampant and, as with many other minorities, the dislike and even hatred is easily seen. African Americans are saddled with persistent racism that is magnified by white privilege. Our task is not just to acknowledge the systemic problems, but to radically affect change.

Humanists have been on the forefront of minority rights, having been instrumental in founding the ACLU, NAACP, NOW, and supporting the fight for reproductive rights. The American Humanist Association was the first national organization to speak out for LGBT rights. Humanists such as Julian Huxley and Eleanor Roosevelt were prominent in the writing of the United Nations Declaration of Human Rights. Our fight for justice must continue.

We must continue to speak to people who suffer inherited disadvantages in race, gender, education and culture: cultures in which, as the philosopher and activist Cornel West said, there is "too much poverty and too little self-love." We need to provide real support to people suffering the inevitable wounds that life imparts. That must include providing both a healing environment and a heroic outlook to help everyone transcend their disadvantages to achieve happier, more meaningful lives.

The writer and politician Sean Faircloth said, "To embrace Humanism is to embrace the concept that caring for others is our highest calling." If that is true, we have so much to do towards ending racism, sexism, homophobia, poverty, global climate change, war, and environmental destruction. Positively, we continue the fight for a woman's right to choose, gender equality, education, reason and all the other factors that benefit all of us.

Humanism has been labeled as anthropocentric and speciesist, guilty of believing human beings are set apart and valued above the rest of creation. If all we are interested in is ourselves, what about other sentient species, other life on earth, and indeed the whole planet? What about sentient artificial intelligence? These situations represent classic ethical dilemmas where we should ask whether human exceptionalism and human-oriented values override consideration of other species.

As we learned earlier, values are often in radical, irresolvable conflict with each other. It appears that this is true here as we try to decide the value of humans versus the rest of the biosphere. At one extreme are some deep ecologists who argue that humans are a destructive weed on the planet. At the other extreme are those that say humans should have dominion over the earth and everything in or on it. While I think a balance of concerns is needed, there isn't an easy answer about where that balance should be.

For an extreme example, ask yourself if it is right for those whose survival depends upon killing an endangered species to be allowed to do so? Arguments about these issues generally center on the idea that humans are not just different in degree, but in kind. Humans are sentient, self-reflective, moral agents. Yet sentience and emotions have also been observed in animals, which have their own inherent value. It is an irresolvable dilemma for which one can find Humanists everywhere across the broad spectrum of arguments. One thing we do know for sure is that animals can suffer. Another is that only humans can really change things.

Since our values come from human values, this warns us that we are always biased towards self-interest. Setting people as the ultimate value can result in making other species and, indeed, the entire biosphere subservient to human needs.

What is clear, however, is that all Humanists highly value nature. Saying Humanists are *only* interested in human welfare misses the point that all of nature is woven into who we are. The only issue is where we should place the balance of our concerns.

We will constantly have to make choices between human welfare and the welfare of other animals. One obvious example: how can we afford to feed a hungry and growing human population without being cruel to livestock or poultry? We will be forced to confront dwindling resources and admit to our excesses. We will have to stop equating progress with mindless growth. We will see that technology cannot always be our savior. We will have to enlarge our minds and hearts while at the same time acknowledging that self-interest is our major driving force. We will have to find ways to extend our altruistic drives, generally reserved for our families and close tribe members, to humanity at large and our biosphere. We will be forced to confront the reality that building a sustainable future inherently means reordering our historic values and concerns. These are not easy tasks, which is why we must garner all the wisdom that understands how our lives are embedded in a planetary environment that we cannot afford to ignore.

Another potential pitfall is overbalancing the use of reason versus issues of the heart. Countless writers have dealt with whether our lives should be governed by our thoughts or our emotions. The danger is that we may become "head only" rationalists on the one hand, or vapid emotionalists on the other. Friedrich Nietzsche saw our lives being driven by what he called the Apollonian and the Dionysian. The Apollonian is the cool, rational, ordered, controlled aspect of our being, while the Dionysian is the wild, uninhibited, emotional, orgiastic sense. A full life balances the two extremes. For a Humanist, the trap is seeing one or the other as the only lifestyle needed for ourselves or others.

This dilemma has been seen historically in the counterbalancing correctives of the Enlightenment and the Romantic movements: the rational versus the emotive or experiential. One need not choose between these poles; Taoists teach us that one can keep them in a dynamic tension. This is represented by the famous Yin Yang symbol. The bottom line is: beware of being all head and no heart on the one hand or, on the other, being a ball of undirected emotions.

Bertrand Russell acknowledged this balanced approach when he said, "The good life is one guided by reason and motivated by love." I think that is the simplest, best description of the Humanist approach to living.

He also said, "To be happy in this world, especially when youth has past, it is necessary to feel oneself not merely an isolated individual whose day will soon be over, but part of the stream of life flowing on from the first germ to the remote and unknown future."

The last danger is to lead your life without an overriding purpose. That is just vapid nihilism. Just because the universe is purposeless, it does not mean that we cannot find our own grand purposes to live a fully human life. In the chapter on meaning, we saw the power of a directed integrated life, one that gives us direction and purpose.

14

How Do We Live A Humanist Life?

"Being a Humanist also means being committed to working for a just society for all. In enabling others to live a free, full life, we create the conditions for a meaningful life for ourselves as well. Through our common efforts, we create the conditions for hope: a hope that is not based on fantasy but on the solid ground of human determination and achievement."
— Ron A. Lindsay, president and CEO of Center for Inquiry

As has been said previously, there is no "right" way to live a Humanist life. There are many ways to live the good life, but some are better than others. Many Christians are living the good life both for themselves and others, and by the same token, many seculars are living rather shallow, disenchanted lives. In any case, I do think that while Humanism isn't the only way to live the good life, overall it is the best way. I wouldn't have devoted my life to it if it were just another optional lifestyle. Humanism is life-affirming rather than life-denying and I feel that joy every day.

It seems we nontheists go by many names, including atheist, secularist, freethinker, Humanist, secular Humanist, rationalist, and agnostic, as if these differences actually mean something. I have heard some imply that there is some sort of ideological difference between these, as if a label automatically locks one into a specific category, but my experience is that the boundaries are quite fluid. I suspect these names are sometimes used more as a marketing tool rather than as having any real inherent meaning.

Still, these names do point toward certain proclivities. Agnostics tend to temper their certainty. Rationalists tend to focus on rational foundations for living. Freethinkers are inclined to address religion's pernicious aspects. Atheists argue against God belief. Humanists tend to focus on the whole life stance that a naturalistic life demands.

The genius of Humanism is that it can be a life stance of heart and mind, reason and compassion. Such a life stance seeks to use all the human tools we have available for creating a secular life. Our efforts to increase our critical intelligence need to be matched by improving our emotional intelligence. The human mind must be seen more like a "committee of the minds" with the rational, emotional, instinctual, behavioral, etc., all competing and interacting. Self-awareness is the starting point for any Humanism.

We come to a nontheistic life stance in many ways. Many have found Humanism by observing the rational incoherence in religion. Many of us have found religion's horrible historical results to be unacceptable. Many can never reconcile the problem of evil in the world. Many of us are motivated by a youthful rebellion. Many feminists, LGBT, and African Americans say they found Humanism through searching for answers to oppression. Experientialists found the aesthetics of nature and our place in it as their motivating force. Many "come-outers" bring an early anger against religion that generally, but not always, matures to dealing with how to live their lives as Humanists. For some of us who were never religious, Humanism just seems normal.

I know of one Humanist, now eighty-eight, who was a Catholic nun until she was forty-one. That was when she took a soft-core pornography book away from a student, read it secretly, masturbated, and had an orgasm for the first time. She said, "I knew right then I wanted to have sex, get married, and leave the church—and I did." Her epiphany about sex led her to question everything she had been told about religion. If they lied to her about sex, what else did they lie to her about? Her questioning led her ultimately to Humanism. So in a very real sense she came to Humanism through pornography and sex! There can be as many different paths to Humanism as there are people.

The way I see it, each of us at one time or another exhibits all the proclivities we see in the nontheistic movement. We all have moments when we are more rational and others when we are more emotional; moments when we are angry about religion and others when we are more tolerant; moments when we desire to be solitary and moments when we want our communities to nurture us; moments when we like the ritual of celebrations and moments when we are more skeptical. We are "both/and" creatures. While having certain proclivities, we are constantly changing, which is why labels of any sort are inherently misleading. We are each a universe in ourselves.

Regardless, our general orientations do matter, and people tend to emphasize one aspect or another. Some of us concentrate on building intentional Humanist communities and others on stomping out the intrusion of church into state. Some of us are drawn to creating a more rational society, while others are drawn to building a more caring society. I don't consider any of the tendencies we follow as ideologies, but more like styles. It's sort of like when we wake up one morning and decide whether today we dress casually in jeans or we dress up . . . or even change later in the day. In the end it really means nothing, as we all ground ourselves in a naturalistic life stance that says this world is all there is. The rest is just style.

I like to see myself as a rather balanced Humanist who rejects extremes in our movement, but when I am honest with myself I know I can flip between being a raving "village atheist" or an incurable romantic. I now think we need all the extremes in our movement, but also a moderate center that grounds us. We need the ardent rationalist to keep society from descending into the never-never land of pseudoscientific nonsense; we need the artists like Kurt Vonnegut and Gene Roddenberry to illuminate how to live our Humanism. We need those who confront religious abuses directly and those who show us how to heal our relationships with our communities at large. We need those who study the intellectual underpinnings of a secular life, and those who show us by example what a lived Humanism looks like. We all have work to do.

We need all the styles of Humanism. Individually, we should not be afraid to wear different style "clothes," some of which initially may not fit us well, but may lead us to a more encompassing, tolerant, generous and, most important, enlightened Humanism. That stylistic flexibility means we can indeed be part of an evolving tradition that evokes the best in us. There are indeed some bad ways to do Humanism, but there is no one "right way" to do Humanism.

Contemplate these comments about our concern for others:

"Humanism involves far more than the negation of supernaturalism. It requires an affirmative philosophy ... translated into a life devoted to one's own improvement and the service of all mankind." – *Corliss Lamont, philosopher and civil libertarian*

"We make a living by what we get. We make a life by what we give." – *Winston Churchill*

Why is it that Humanists put so much emphasis on caring and doing for others? Why should we see caring for others as our highest calling? Humanism has sometimes been described as attempting to widen our circles of compassion. Why should we devote ourselves to "the service of all mankind?" Why should we turn our attention to others over ourselves?

Wise people throughout the ages have spoken of service to others as a path to wholeness and happiness for ourselves. After our own initial needs are met, we gain so much happiness and meaning in our life if we can get beyond our own egos and needs and reach out to help others. Science now indicates that helping others is a road to emotional wellness. It is easy to see why. It's not just that we increase the overall good, but we ennoble ourselves and others.

John Dewey, one of the greatest American Humanists, placed great value on our social selves. He said, "The things in civilization we most prize are not of ourselves. They exist by grace of the doings and sufferings of the continuous human community in which we are a link. Ours is the responsibility of conserving, transmitting, rectifying, and expanding the heritage of values we have received that those who come after us may receive it more solid and secure, more widely accessible and more generously shared than we have received it."

In the chapter on religion, we started a conversation about the need in all of us for an overarching story of life. Humanism offers this alternative story.

We can argue until the end of time about the inherent contradictions in the Bible, the pernicious effects of religion, and the logic of Darwinism and not win people over unless their fears are answered. People who are drawn to religion for non-rational reasons are unlikely to be swayed by rational arguments. Religion understands that people long for a whole, unified story that quells their fears and their existential angst. Sometimes, it seems to me, we Humanists need a voice that is more evocative than rational and strident.

In marketing it is said that it is not the features that sell a product, but the benefits. We need to sing a song of praise to the glories of nature, the immediacy of love in our finite lives, and being part of a community of hearts that seek the affirmation of each person's equal worth and dignity. Our joys come when we smell freedom's lilac scent, relentlessly pursue progressive truth, become excited over finding that truth, calm ourselves in the caress of compassion, and lock arms in democratic solidarity. We truly live when we faint in the arms of love, seek justice, laugh in surprise at wonder, find inner peace in quiet moments, and dance to life's rhythms.

This is Humanism's imperative for all of us: tell this story of ours. Provide a forward-looking Humanism that encompasses all it means to be human.

Humanism gives us an alternative story on how to live. For example, Humanism sees sex as a great joy, something to be celebrated, not suppressed, controlled, or a source of shame. Attempts to control sex and particularly women's bodies permeate all of religion. In our case, the morality of sex is limited to whether the adult persons involved are in consensual non-coercive agreement and treat each other with respect. It is one more example of how we can live our lives exuberantly. Nietzsche said he couldn't believe in a God that didn't know how to dance. We know how to dance.

- Humanism reminds us of the need for courage—courage to face adversity with grace and confidence.
- Humanism reminds us of the need to fight for justice for all.
- Humanism reminds us that beliefs matter and that we have an ethical responsibility to get to the truth of things.
- Humanism reminds us that our heart matters as much as our head. How we embrace love, compassion and sympathy makes a huge difference.
- Humanism reminds us that we are all imbedded in society and have responsibilities to the social fabric that nurtures us.

- Humanism reminds us that there are always those suffering alone on the margins of society and that our duty is towards improving their welfare.

Why are you reading this? I think it is because we both want a better world. We want a better world, but we believe that secular values, indeed Humanist values, will make that better world. This isn't just about the "rightness" of our cause, but about its practical effects. Even still, there is something more.

Our hearts long for an integrated whole view of life, where our ideals match reality. We long for a vital center to our lives that both grounds us and inspires us, a vision of grander authenticity to our lives, not just smaller truths. All of us long for an evocative whole story and a higher vision that lifts our hearts, moves our society, pushes us to higher meanings, and ennobles our lives. Some may find that integrated story is already with us, in the balanced Humanist secular life of here and now, as we accept the exhilarating challenge of a responsible search for truth and meaning.

The Humanist life stance is based on values, not our beliefs. They encompass open-minded critical thinking, science, justice, freedom, tolerance, democracy, reason, compassion, human rights, all people's inherent worth and dignity, and the importance of human flourishing. These are the values that hold our web of belief together.

We can't afford the luxury of just critiquing religion. We must tell our alternative story so anyone contemplating change will know a non-religious worldview can support, inspire, and comfort them; that knowledge of science, while tentative, is surely firmer than blind faith;

that the exhilaration of focusing on the here and now is more meaningful than otherworldliness; that hope and love are certainly better than hate and divisiveness; that compassion and responsibility can be balanced with self-interest and freedom. The ambiguity inherent in all our value/ethical/political choices need not paralyze us; it does make it even more important that we reflectively consider all our choices.

Humanist ethics derives its power from affirming all people's inherent worth and dignity. It realizes that, if justice is to be given, only we can give it. If love is to be given, only we have that power in this moment and in this hour. Real suffering exists and only we can bind the wounds. This world certainly is all and enough—enough to fill us with the joy, wonder, hope and awe that is our natural birthright.

Now is our time. Now is our chance to move society toward reason and the good life. Now is our time to move society out of the dark ages of theocratic and ideological control and toward human fulfillment. We cannot falter in the face of certain hostility or our own inherent ambiguity; neither can we stand idly by hoping for a secular society to automatically shape itself. It is our duty to show that a secular world need not end in nihilism. It is our obligation to demonstrate that we can build communities that embrace a progressive, ethical, Humanist worldview of human and global good.

15

Final Words

For all the talk about reason and science, Humanism is really a passionate love affair. It is a love affair with life in the here and now, not some mythical hereafter. Humanism is a love affair with a progressive vision of civilization where each of us can add to our growing library of wisdom, our evolving knowledge of what is and what is truly important. None of history's great achievements would have been possible without a love for the adventure of learning and creating a better life. We have great cultural achievements in science, art, music, literature, philosophy, history, psychology, and political thought, which all inform each other, that have been born of that long Humanist tradition.

People of both a secular and a religious mindset today have retreated from grander ideas to mere inward, personal meanings and purposes. The idea that civilization was continuously progressing was challenged by the horrors of the Holocaust, world wars and instances where reason turned against itself as a tool for power and control. We fear "Grand Narratives," labels, and larger stories of how life is and could be. We live in a cynical, narcissistic age without vision. Our retreat from community and larger commitments has sapped our passions. I think it is time to reevaluate and move beyond these fears.

For centuries, Humanists have overcome huge barriers and, as a result, have made a real difference in the world. They never would have succeeded except for their passion for truth, for justice, for mercy, and for making the world in some way a little bit better.

Humanism is merely that ongoing evolving life stance that challenges us beyond simple atheism, beyond our own self-centeredness, and beyond our own fear of larger commitments. The challenge is to embrace the best of what we and society can be. We have a statement of our vison in the *Humanist Manifesto lll*. Not a rigid doctrinaire statement, it is a consensus that continues to evolve over time. Its purpose is to help people understand what they can believe when they don't believe in God. Even so, it is merely a jumping-off point for the real, ongoing quest.

Some have neglected to use the full breadth of Humanism's resources. Some would see science answering everything we need to know, ignoring the many tools the humanities have given us. Democracy and the concepts of human rights are gifts from history and civilization. Philosophy gives us tools for critical thinking and a conceptual framework to evaluate the world. Literature and art heighten our awareness about what values are important. As Curtis Reese, one if the founders of modern-day Humanism, said, we must relate to others in a purposeful fashion to "weave the best personal values into a noble social order."

All human beings seek a whole integrated story for our lives, something that gives us power and meaning, hope, joy and purpose. This deep identification of all people's shared values is what Humanism offers beyond just atheism. Most of us privately long for something worthy of our noblest devotion. Paul Kurtz wrote his book, *The Transcendental Temptation*, as a warning about the temptation of irrational, other-worldly visions. Yet his whole life reflected a Promethean urge toward a transcendent Humanist vision of how we might work toward the moral ideal.

In our troubled anti-foundational times, I think it's time once again to look beyond society's failings, the universe's inherent meaninglessness, our own needs, and our avoidance of grand purposes. Instead, we should once again look toward the heart's commitments to the best of who we and society can be. Being a Humanist takes passion, courage and commitment. It requires a love of life that can help us rise above our age's vacuous, cynical malaise and empower us with a vision of what a Humanistic society would look like.

Humanism at its best offers a grander vision of life. It is a devotion to humanity and the biosphere that we are part of. It is our passionate commitment to the best ideals that are supported by what experience, science, and civilization have taught us. That vision tells us Humanism is larger than any of us. I believe we have a duty to continue Humanism's evolving tradition, which has inspired countless individuals to make the world better. At the same time, it motivates us to fill our lives with transcendent purpose, to live a meaningful, exuberant life—a life worth living.

The Author

The author, Michael Werner, is president of the Humanist Foundation and past president of the American Humanist Association. He is a scientist, philosopher and businessman. He has worked in many social action causes. Early on he devoted his life to Humanism and it has meant everything to him.

Bibliography

Best primers

Cave, Peter. *Humanism: A Beginner's Guide*. London: Oneworld Publications, 2009.

Roy Speckhardt. *Creating Change Through Humanism*. Washington DC: Humanist Press, 2015.

Einstein, Albert. *Essays in Humanism*. New York: Philosophical Library, 1950, 1983.

Epstein, Greg. *Good Without God: What a Billion Nonreligious People Do Believe*. New York: HarperCollins, 2010.

Ericson, E. L. "Ethical Humanism." In *The Humanist Alternative*, edited by Paul Kurtz, 56-57. Buffalo, New York: Prometheus Books, 1973.

Herrick, Jim. *Humanism: An Introduction*. Buffalo, New York: Prometheus Books, 2005.

Humanist Manifesto III. Available online at the American Humanist Association. https://americanhumanist.org/what-is-humanism/manifesto3/

Kurtz, Paul. *Eupraxophy: Living Without Religion*. Buffalo, New York: Prometheus Books, 1989.

Lamont, Corliss. *The Philosophy of Humanism*. New York: The Continuum Publishing Company, 1990.

Law, Stephen, *Humanism*. Oxford: Oxford University Press, 2011.

Morain, Lloyd and Morain, Mary. *Humanism — The Next Step*. Washington: Humanist Press, 1998.

Murry, William R. *Reason and Reverence*. Boston: Skinner House Books, 2007

Murry, William R. *Becoming More Fully Human*. Hamden, Connecticut: Religious Humanism Press, 2011.

Vail, C.W. *Thus Let Me Live*. An Essay in Humanism. Sarasota, Florida: First Design Publishing Inc., 2014.

Historical

Dietrich, John. *Ten Sermons*. Fellowship of Religious Humanists, 1989

"A Humanist Manifesto." *The New Humanist*, VI, May/June (1933): 3:1-5. Available online at the American Humanist Association. https://americanhumanist.org/what-is-humanism/manifesto1/

"Humanist Manifesto II," *The Humanist*, XXIII, September/October (1973): 5:4-9. Available online at the American Humanist Association. https://americanhumanist.org/what-is-humanism/manifesto2/

Maslow, Abraham H. *Religions, Values, and Peak Experiences*. Columbus, OH: Ohio State University Press, 1964.

Potter, Charles Francis. *Humanism: A New Religion*. New York: Simon and Schuster, 1930.

Reese, Curtis W. *Humanism*. Chicago: Open Court Publishing Company, 1926.

Schiller, F. C. S. *Humanism: Philosophical Essays*. New York: The Macmillan Company, 1903.

Schultz, William. *Making the Manifesto: A History of Early Religious Humanism*. Chicago: Meadville/Lombard Theological School doctoral dissertation, 1975.

Sellars, Roy Wood. *The Next Step in Religion*. New York: The Macmillan Company, 1918.

Wilson, Edwin H. *The Genesis of a Humanist Manifesto*. Edited by Teresa Maciocha. Amherst, NY: Humanist Press, 1995.

APPENDIX 1

Humanist Manifesto III

HUMANISM AND ITS ASPIRATIONS

Humanism is a progressive philosophy of life that, without supernaturalism, affirms our ability and responsibility to lead ethical lives of personal fulfillment that aspire to the greater good of humanity.

The lifestance of Humanism—guided by reason, inspired by compassion, and informed by experience—encourages us to live life well and fully. It evolved through the ages and continues to develop through the efforts of thoughtful people who recognize that values and ideals, however carefully wrought, are subject to change as our knowledge and understandings advance.

This document is part of an ongoing effort to manifest in clear and positive terms the conceptual boundaries of Humanism, not what we must believe but a consensus of what we do believe. It is in this sense that we affirm the following:

Knowledge of the world is derived by observation, experimentation, and rational analysis. Humanists find that science is the best method for determining this knowledge as well as for solving problems and developing beneficial technologies. We also recognize the value of new departures in thought, the arts, and inner experience—each subject to analysis by critical intelligence.

Humans are an integral part of nature, the result of unguided evolutionary change. Humanists recognize nature as self-existing. We accept our life as all and enough, distinguishing things as they are from things as we might wish or imagine them to be. We welcome the challenges of the future, and are drawn to and undaunted by the yet to be known.

Ethical values are derived from human need and interest as tested by experience. Humanists ground values in human welfare shaped by human circumstances, interests, and concerns and extended to the global ecosystem and beyond. We are committed to treating each person as having inherent worth and dignity, and to making informed choices in a context of freedom consonant with responsibility.

Life's fulfillment emerges from individual participation in the service of humane ideals. We aim for our fullest possible development and animate our lives with a deep sense of purpose, finding wonder and awe in the joys and beauties of human existence, its challenges and tragedies, and even in the inevitability and finality of death. Humanists rely on the rich heritage of human culture and the lifestance of Humanism to provide comfort in times of want and encouragement in times of plenty.

Humans are social by nature and find meaning in relationships. Humanists long for and strive toward a world of mutual care and concern, free of cruelty and its consequences, where differences are resolved cooperatively without resorting to violence. The joining of individuality with interdependence enriches our lives, encourages us to enrich the lives of others, and inspires hope of attaining peace, justice, and opportunity for all.

Working to benefit society maximizes individual happiness. Progressive cultures have worked to free humanity from the brutalities of mere survival and to reduce suffering, improve society, and develop global community. We seek to minimize the inequities of circumstance and ability, and we support a just distribution of nature's resources and the fruits of human effort so that as many as possible can enjoy a good life.

Humanists are concerned for the well being of all, are committed to diversity, and respect those of differing yet humane views. We work to uphold the equal enjoyment of human rights and civil liberties in an open, secular society and maintain it is a civic duty to participate in the democratic process and a planetary duty to protect nature's integrity, diversity, and beauty in a secure, sustainable manner.

Thus engaged in the flow of life, we aspire to this vision with the informed conviction that humanity has the ability to progress toward its highest ideals. The responsibility for our lives and the kind of world in which we live is ours and ours alone.

For historical purposes, see Humanist Manifestos: I and II.

Humanist Manifesto is a trademark of the American Humanist Association. © 2003 *American Humanist Association*

APPENDIX 2

Robert Ingersoll's Vow

When I became convinced that the Universe is natural—
that all the ghosts and gods are myths, there entered into
my brain, into my soul, into every drop of my blood, the
sense, the feeling, the joy of freedom. The walls of my
prison crumbled and fell, the dungeon was flooded with
light, and all the bolts, and bars, and manacles became
dust. I was no longer a servant, a serf, or a slave. There
was for me no master in all the wide world—not even
in infinite space. I was free—free to think, to express my
thoughts—free to live to my own ideal—free to live for
myself and those I loved—free to use all my faculties, all
my senses—free to spread imagination's wings—free to
investigate, to guess and dream and hope—free to judge
and determine for myself—free to reject all ignorant and
cruel creeds, all the "inspired" books that savages have
produced, and all the barbarous legends of the past—
free from popes and priests—free from all the "called"
and "set apart" —free from sanctified mistakes and holy
lies—free from the fear of eternal pain—free from the
winged monsters of the night—free from devils, ghosts,

and gods. For the first time I was free. There were no prohibited places in all the realms of thought—no air, no space, where fancy could not spread her painted wings—no chains for my limbs—no lashes for my back—no fires for my flesh—no master's frown or threat—no following another's steps—no need to bow, or cringe, or crawl, or utter lying words. I was free. I stood erect and fearlessly, joyously, faced all worlds.

And then my heart was filled with gratitude, with thankfulness, and went out in love to all the heroes, the thinkers who gave their lives for the liberty of hand and brain—for the freedom of labor and thought—to those who fell in the fierce fields of war, to those who died in dungeons bound with chains—to those who proudly mounted scaffold's stairs—to those whose bones were crushed, whose flesh was scarred and torn—to those by fire consumed—to all the wise, the good, the brave of every land, whose thoughts and deeds have given freedom to the sons of men. And then I vowed to grasp the torch that they had held, and hold it high, that light might conquer darkness still.

– Robert G. Ingersoll (1833-1899)

APPENDIX 3

Critical Thinking / Supportive thinking

In Chapter 5 we considered various ways to gain knowledge that people say they have found. All have limitations and some, like divine revelation, are worthless. We have a number of critical thinking tools to use in our search for the truth, no matter what methods we are using. These are quick, proven tests to see if we are on the right track and to narrow down our search.

I have compiled a list of critical thinking do's and don'ts. Here are some of the best:

Critical Thinking Do's

- Keep an open mind.
- Don't be trapped into absolute certainty.
- Never forget that we are all biased and are blind to it.
- Ask yourself if you are giving a reason or a rationalization.
- Have the courage to change your mind in the light of new evidence.

- Use Occam's razor—a rule of thumb that tells us to generally choose the simplest alternative with the fewest assumptions when faced with two or more hypotheses.
- Always seek independent analysis and confirmation.
- Generally the best hypothesis is the one that is the most conservative, that is, the one that best fits with established beliefs and expert opinion.
- We have good reason to doubt a proposition if it conflicts with other propositions that we have good reason to believe.
- We should accept an extraordinary hypothesis only if no ordinary one will do.
- Quantify your data wherever possible.
- Aggressively look for alternative hypotheses to your propositions.
- Develop proposals to falsify your proposition. It is almost always possible and required.
- We are justified in believing a proposition when we have no reason to doubt it.
- Get an independent review of the facts.
- Remember that for some things there is no answer, and that's OK.
- Many times we are left with ambiguity. Deal with it.
- Do use arguments that are coherent and consistent with past knowledge unless there are substantial reasons not to.

Critical Thinking Don'ts

- Don't attack the person's character, but the argument itself. ("*Ad hominem*")

- Don't misrepresent, exaggerate or add onto a person's arguments in order to make them easier to attack. ("Straw man fallacy")
- Don't use small numbers to represent the whole. ("Hasty generalization")
- Don't claim that because something occurred before something else, it must be the cause. (*"Post hoc*/false cause")
- Don't reduce the argument down to two possibilities. ("False dichotomy")
- Don't argue that because of our ignorance, a proposition must be true or false. (*"Ad ignorantiam"*)
- Don't lay the burden of proof onto the person questioning the claim. ("Burden of proof reversal")
- Don't assume "this" follows "that," when "it" has no logical connection. (*"Non sequitur"*)
- Don't claim that because a proposition is popular, therefore, it must be true. ("Bandwagon fallacy")
- Don't appeal to an authority to support a proposition. ("Appeal to authority")
- Don't claim moral authority over others. ("Moral high ground fallacy")
- Don't argue that we can't believe in something because bad things will happen if we do. ("Argument from adverse consequences"
- Don't assume the answer in support of the claim. ("Begging the question")
- Don't pick only the data that supports your view. ("Cherry picking" or "Confirmation bias")
- Don't use an argument showing how something was caused after something else occurred. (*"Post hoc, ergo*

propter hoc"—Latin for "It happened after, so it was caused by")

- Don't confuse correlation with causation. ("Correlation is not causation")
- Don't claim that whatever has not been proven false must be true. ("Appeal to ignorance")
- Don't argue from extremes, ignoring the middle ground. ("Excluded middle," or "False dichotomy")
- Don't use lousy statistics. ("Statistics can lie")
- Don't believe something is real because it is logically possible. ("Imaginary possibilities")
- Don't believe something is false just because it hasn't been conclusively refuted or proven. ("Quick dismissal fallacy")
-

Supportive Thinking

We can become a one-trick pony, being really great critical thinkers and ignoring other modes of thinking and behavior. Critical thinking is crucial for discovering truth, but if we overuse criticism in our interpersonal lives we can become, frankly, just critical jerks. Another quality is equally important in our daily lives, known as emotional intelligence. That term, as popularized by the American psychologist Daniel Goleman, represents "the ability of individuals to recognize their own and other people's emotions, to discriminate between different feelings and label them appropriately, and to use emotional information to guide thinking and behavior."

A favorite joke among social activists is a line the cartoonist Charles Schultz used in one of his *Peanuts* comic strips: "I love humanity, it's people I can't stand." Each of us in our own lives knows people who truly love others and are both happier and more successful than others. They easily forgive others, try to find the best in people, and are warm and embracing of everyone. They are charitable and empathetic. They perceptively understand people. They live better lives and produce better results for everyone.

I have seen my mother-in-law, who totally accepted children and grandchildren when they had life problems. I watched their faces glow in the awareness that she truly gave them unconditional love. She was an island of safety in a turbulent sea. But eventually these children grew up and changed. It would have been so easy for her to use critical intelligence and chastise them, but she was wiser, more patient, and understanding. This is just one example of the power of trust, supportive intelligence, and love.

CPSIA information can be obtained
at www.ICGtesting.com
Printed in the USA
FFOW03n2039210318
45942941-46844FF